THE HOLY WILL
OF GOD

THE HOLY WILL OF GOD

SOURCE OF PEACE AND HAPPINESS

by

Rev. Leo Pyzalski, C.SS.R.

"The Lord gave, and the Lord hath taken away. . . blessed be the name of the Lord." —Job 1:21

TAN BOOKS AND PUBLISHERS, INC.
Rockford, Illinois 61105

Imprimi Potest: A. M. Gearin, C.SS.R.
                     Provincial Superior
                     Brooklyn, New York
                     October 8, 1946

Nihil Obstat: William Joseph Schreck
                     Censor Deputatus

Imprimatur: ✠ John F. O'Hara, C.S.C.
                     Bishop of Buffalo

Originally published by Holy Legion Office, Sacred Heart Villa, Park Ridge, Illinois.

ISBN: 0-89555-411-9

Library of Congress Catalog Card No.: 90-71554

Printed and bound in the United States of America.

TAN BOOKS AND PUBLISHERS, INC.
P. O. Box 424
Rockford, Illinois 61105

1991

"Whatsoever shall befall the just man, it shall not make him sad."

—*Proverbs* 12:21

CONTENTS

FOREWORD

The great Doctor of the Church St. Alphonsus Liguori has enriched spiritual literature, among his other compositions, with a short, charming Italian poem about the Will of God. Every stanza of this mystical jewel ends with the exclamation:

> *Quanto degna sei d'amore,*
> *O Divina Volonta!*
> *How lovable thou art,*
> *O Holy Will of God!*

These simple but seraphic words are an accurate expression, not only of the very core of the soul of St. Alphonsus, but of the feelings of all Saints of God on earth and in Heaven.

There never was a Saint and never can be one whose attitude toward the Divine Will is lukewarm, since love of the Will of God constitutes the very essence of sanctity.

Instinctively, every fervent soul who takes its sanctification seriously feels attracted to the Holy Will of God, and sooner or later develops a real devotion to this Holy Will.

Any kind of perfection or sanctity which is

not closely related to the Will of God, and does not result in increasing love of the Divine Will, should be branded as superficial, doubtful, if not illusory.

Real and profound devotion to God's Holy Will is always the fruit of earnest and persevering endeavor, of continual prayer and of a very abundant grace of the Holy Spirit. Many souls called to perfection never attain that supreme goal of the spiritual life, since they lack the courage to cooperate with the grace of God. Indeed, it takes enormous courage to embrace—always and everywhere—in all details of life, the Holy Will of God.

At the same time, however, tender love toward the Divine Will is a guarantee of celestial peace and happiness. Yea, this love is the only way to genuine and permanent happiness.

These and similar reasons have prompted the author to publish the present treatise.

He humbly entreats his Holy Father Alphonsus to obtain for him and for all readers of this booklet—through the intercession of Mary Immaculate and through the infinite merits of Jesus—a seraphic love toward the Holy Will of God.

Jesus, Mary, Joseph, Alphonsus — deign to assist my poor endeavors!

—The Author
Buffalo, August 2, 1946

THE SPIRIT OF THE WICKED WORLD

Life on earth seems charming, particularly to younger people who have not as yet been made acquainted with failures, trials, mishaps and sufferings. With time, however, all children of the world are disappointed in their hunt for true happiness. They realize the indubitable fact that there are more thorns than roses in human life.

At least ninety-nine percent of the worldlings feel discontented, and many of them are utterly unhappy. Why? Because they have taken the wrong road to happiness.

What is the spirit of the world? What is the leading idea of its life and strivings? An easy-going existence, absolute freedom in every regard, complete independence, even from God and His eternal laws. In other words, man wants to be like God...in a wrong sense.

Meanwhile, peace and happiness are in store for man in humble submission to the eternal, immutable, infinitely adorable Will of his Creator. To tread the road to happiness, man must recognize his true condition, which is one of absolute dependence on God, and consequently, of complete dependence on God's representatives on earth, as well. To feel and to see things otherwise means to put oneself in a false position, and thus to deprive oneself of real happiness.

Freedom?...Yes—man can and should have it as far as it proves essential to permanent happiness. All depends, however, upon the kind of freedom he covets. If he insists upon his alleged right to follow his natural inclinations, his likes and dislikes in everything, though he knows and feels that his nature is more prone to evil than to good, then he gradually draws away from God, the eternal source of true happiness. The only kind of freedom that becomes Christians and results in real happiness is the "freedom of the children of God." It means freedom—real, perfect freedom—within the limits of Divine law, Divine Will.

Alas, the vast majority of mankind discard this genuine freedom since it is connected with self-control, with many acts of self-denial, and with solid virtue. They prefer unlimited freedom, not excepting the freedom to offend God. Is it a wonder, then, that peace and happiness have almost completely disappeared from our earth, so as to make it a real valley of tears?

Godless people are wont to complain that human life is only too often like Hell. They fail, however, to explain that they themselves are building and shaping that earthly hell, while revolting against the Maker of Heaven and earth and disregarding His commandments, insulting His Infinite Majesty or even denying His very existence. Yes, earthly life undoubtedly is a clear prelude to Hell, once people forget their Father in Heaven, since there is no perfect justice here below and never will be, on account of the basic imperfection of human nature, and much more as a result of Original Sin.

We hear at times about the "mystery of evil" on earth. Indeed, there is so much bad will in human souls, such general wickedness in mankind, as to make us wonder again and again about these regrettable dispositions of the human heart. Why are most people so blind as to obstinately follow their bad inclinations and passions, though experience has taught them so often that this is not the way to real happiness? Why do some people revolt against God in such an insolent manner as to resemble Satan and his followers? Can they delude themselves that peace and happiness will be found in opposition to the Almighty Creator? Do they not know, or at least surmise—if they are unbelievers or ignorant people—that soon, upon crossing the threshold of eternity, they will have to face the infinite justice of God's tribunal?

How pitiable the future fate of sinners! Instead of the absolute, unlimited freedom they were demanding and pursuing on earth, they will find in eternity the most excruciating bondage. For, Hell is a prison, the most terrible prison, in comparison with which earthly penitentiaries seem like comfortable, delightful apartments. Followers of the wicked world! Why are you so thoughtless and unreasonable?

In the face of that deplorable wickedness of the world which consists essentially in revolt against the Holy Will of God, souls of good will should all the more beware of every shadow of opposition against the Divine Will. Let us be rather suspicious of everything that originates in the wicked world. Certainly, no one, not even religious souls who live in the seclusion of a convent, are immune from the poisoned spirit of the world.

The mere fact of living in this wicked world is not dangerous in itself, since Divine grace can enable a soul to serve God faithfully and even to attain a high degree of sanctity, in the midst of sinners, and in the very atmosphere of Hell. What exposes souls to the greatest peril is their light-mindedness, their naive and thoughtless trust in modern opinions, in fashionable theories. Only too often people forget about the maxim that "not all that glitters is gold."

THE SPIRIT OF SELF-WILL MAY INVADE RELIGIOUS COMMUNITIES

Religious souls are not of this world. In consequence of their profession they belong entirely to God, and bear the title and dignity of spouses of Jesus Christ. They are living, however, in the midst of the wicked world and breathe its foul atmosphere. It is, then, no wonder that traces of the spirit of the world, of excessive self-assertion, of pride and self-will are now and again noticeable even in convents.

The modern social structure, the relations between classes in human society, and between individuals, become more and more democratic, as the doctrine of human equality is repeatedly stressed. Undoubtedly, this is a desirable phenomenon. Sound democracy is essentially Christian. Was not Jesus Christ, who so often called Himself "The Son of Man" while in fact one with His heavenly Father in Divinity, infinitely more democratic than any social or religious worker known in history?

Yet, democracy can be misunderstood. Besides,

democracy may not be applied unreservedly in religious life. The latter is based upon supernatural foundations. It refers directly to God. And God is infinite Majesty, whereas man is as dust and nothingness before Him.

The constitution of Holy Church bears some democratic traits. It emphasizes the equality of all human beings, of all races, in a more definite manner than any other institution or philosophy on earth. But the relationship of the Church with its members is by no means democratic in the human and modern sense of the term. Holy Church is the Mystical Body of Christ. It is called the Bride of the Divine Lamb Jesus. It is our Mother in Christ, we are its children. Its authority to teach and to govern us is that of Christ Himself. In other words, the constitution of Holy Church has more in common with theocracy than with democracy.

Accordingly, the whole life of religious communities, that are parts of the Church and tend unto the same end of saving and sanctifying souls, must be governed by supernatural, Divine principles. Every detail of that life is supposed to be related to God's glory and love. Those trusted with leadership and administration of religious communities are vested with Divine authority, since they are appointed representatives of God. Hence, the attitude of subjects is expected to be one of sincere and humble deference and childlike docility toward all legitimate Superiors. This is something quite different from modern democracy.

People who join a religious order are perfectly aware of the way of life they choose for themselves, since they are adequately instructed about the difference between secular and religious customs and laws pending their preparation for the new kind of life. So they renounce in advance all claims to democratic participation in the administration and spiritual guidance of the whole religious body. They consciously sacrifice their personal liberty, their own will, to please God and to render Him more glory.

However, it is much easier to declare one's willingness to live and to die under such supernatural laws, than to make good that promise day by day, at almost any moment and under all circumstances. Human nature never gives up in its struggle against Divine grace. Thus, even religious animated with the best intentions may at times deviate more or less from the narrow path of Divine Will, to follow a more comfortable line—under various and specious pretexts.

Particularly, in our day of ultra-democratic tendencies is this likely to happen and, indeed, does happen frequently. Self-will takes the place of humble and cheerful obedience. As long as Superiors adjust their directions to the likes and dislikes of their subjects, they are praised and

cherished and obeyed promptly. Whenever the
contrary occurs, they will be blamed, at least
very often, of imprudence, ruthlessness or lack
of charity. Allegedly, Superiors forget that all
members of the community have the same rights
since they are bound by the same religious
profession.

Now the first and most essential task of every
religious community is the imitation of Our Lord
Jesus Christ. Social, educational or similar work
is not the supreme task of religious life. It is
only a means to further God's glory. This supreme goal is attained in a twofold manner: A
religious must above all follow in the footsteps
of Jesus, the Divine Exemplar of perfection and
sanctity, and must, secondly, lead and help others
to shape their thinking, feeling and acting upon
that supreme and Divine Model. To perform any
social work whatsoever without regarding God's
glory and the teachings of Jesus Christ, the Supreme Master of mankind, would be incompat-
ible with religious obligations and the religious
character in general.

Let us, then, "render to Caesar the things that
are Caesar's, and to God the things that are
God's." (*Matt.* 22:21). Let us with society in
general enjoy our modern democratic customs
and laws in worldly affairs—without forgetting,
however, that the religious life is not of this
world, and consequently cannot be based upon

democratic rules in the common sense of the term. True, religious communities and Holy Church herself apply some democratic principles in their administration, but only as far as is possible without spoiling the conception of evangelical perfection and without lessening the childlike attitude of souls toward the representatives of God.

Wherever in religious communities these worldly tendencies gain the upper hand, and visibly impair the childlike deference and obedience to all legitimate Superiors, there the supernatural spirit and real religious sanctity will be on the decline. Unless this worldly trend is stopped in time, it will become harder and harder to govern the order, to keep observance, to maintain real striving for perfection. After losing the spirit of Christ, which is one of filial docility toward God and His representatives, a religious order is but a poor makeshift of what it ought to be. It cannot expect the Divine blessings on its activities, nor real happiness in its members.

What every community greatly needs is sound conservatism. Even the welfare of the ordinary society is endangered unless it has some conservative elements. This conservatism will prevent hasty, violent and unreasonable changes in ordinary life, in social relations, as well as in politics. The religious life must all the more be based on conservatism, since its constitution originates in the Holy Gospel, the immutable code of virtue, of perfection and of sanctity. New forms of following the evangelical counsels may be adopted in the course of time, but the basic principle of a childlike attitude toward God and His representatives in the religious life must remain untouched. It is the vital core of religious sanctity.

– 3 –

THE WILL OF GOD IN THEORY
AND IN PRACTICE

No doubt, all religious are unanimous in theoretically accepting the Holy Will of God as the supreme, unalterable rule of their lives. They sorely resent every charge of opposition against the Divine Will. And yet, how small is the number of religious souls who wholeheartedly embrace the Will of God in all its details all through their lives. To do so means great sanctity. And it is only the very few who reach such heights of sanctity.

To agree with the principle that God's Will must be and must remain forever the absolutely immutable law for those dedicated to the service of God, is very simple and easy. It is achieved in religion by all those souls who do not consciously revolt against God. The greatest difficulty, however, in the practical striving for religious sanctity consists in subduing one's self to the Will of God.

Many religious are living in a state of voluntary or semi-voluntary self-delusion. They believe and feel that they are in perfect accord with the Will of God, because they accept and revere, or even love that Holy Will in theory. Undoubtedly, such an inner disposition is meritorious before God. It amounts even to a certain degree of perfection. But it is a mistake to identify this laudable attitude toward the Divine Will with truly great sanctity, which requires a practical, unwavering and tender love for all the demands and wishes of the Will of God. At times, even religious quite unfaithful to their holy obligations, especially in matters of obedience, manage to convince themselves that they love God's Will. How can they amend when they imagine themselves so innocent and perfect? What a sad awakening for them on the Day of Judgment!

It is, therefore, of extreme importance to be very critical with oneself in matters of submission to the Divine Will and the Divine Complacency. Never let us forget that real, practical union of our will with the Will of God in everything is the most difficult task we have to achieve upon the way to religious sanctity. As a rule, it takes many years to make progress on this royal road. Besides, assiduous cooperation with the grace of God is indispensable. Half-hearted, lukewarm efforts will not bring us very far.

The striving after final and perfect union of our will with the Will of God must begin with the firm resolution, often repeated before God, to seek always and everywhere, God's glory and complacency by complying with all the wishes of His Fatherly Heart. "Thy Will be done" should be a very frequent ejaculation of souls striving after evangelical perfection. The simple desire to do God's Will is not tantamount to the real habit of complying in everything with the Divine complacency. The soul's courage in applying its sublime resolutions may fail at times. Nevertheless, repeated good resolutions strengthen our will, and certainly are very meritorious for Heaven. They draw down upon the soul a great abundance of Divine grace.

To make our basic resolution of complying unreservedly with God's Will more sincere, more effective and practical, a thorough knowledge of that Adorable Will and its relation to the human will is very desirable. For, no one is able to love ardently what he does not know or with which he is acquainted only superficially.

Let us consider here at least the fundamental truths concerning the Divine Will as far as it constitutes the rule of human life.

The Holy Will of God encompasses, so to say, our whole existence in time and in eternity, and refers to every detail of that existence. In other words, Divine plans for our life, our salvation and sanctification, were elaborated from Eternity to a degree which is possible only to Divine Omniscience and Wisdom. Not one detail

is completely left to our self-will. True, we are
in possession of a free will and may use it,
provided, however, we remain within the limits
of God's good pleasure. Otherwise, we misuse
our God-given liberty, and deserve punishment.

Many human actions are regarded by theologians as morally indifferent, neither good nor
bad, as for instance an innocent play, a relaxa-
tion, a pastime one enjoys for diversion. But even
these actions must be referred at least in a general
way, virtually and implicitly, to the glory of God
and God's good pleasure. Since no creature is
in any way independent of its Maker, hence no
conscious and deliberate action can be performed
in the spirit of absolute independence from the
Divine Will. God alone is absolutely independent in His existence and in His works.

This inevitable and absolute dependence of our
whole being and doing on God, does not in any
sense whatever destroy or impair our free will.
On the contrary, the latter is safeguarded and
perfected in the same measure as it complies with
the eternal and most holy Will of God.

The all-encompassing Will of God, as the supreme and immutable rule of all human actions,
should not be a source of uneasiness and continual anxiety for people of good will. It is true,
very often we are not able to realize and ascertain what the real, objective Will of God is. Even
the opinions of prudent and enlightened men

whom we may consult are at times divided as
to certain aspects of God's good pleasure. So
it is quite possible that we are often mistaken
in what we believe to be God's Holy Will. Is
not this fact extremely distressing to souls who
long for nothing else on earth than lovingly
doing the Will of God?

No, they have no reason to worry. For, whenever theology states and emphasizes that perfection and sanctity essentially consist in lovingly
doing God's Will, it means not so much the objective Will of God as what we sincerely believe
to be the Will of God. Of course, no soul striving for perfection may rely upon itself. It is supposed to ask for advice of its Superiors or
spiritual guides in doubtful matters. But whenever there is no chance to seek advice as time
presses, and the soul decides to do what it believes to be in accord with God's good pleasure,
undoubtedly it is complying with the Will of
God. That is to say, God wants us to do at all
moments of our life what we sincerely believe
to be His real Will. He certainly will not take
amiss or punish our inevitable mistakes concerning His objective good pleasure.

Only those who indulge in conceited self-
confidence, although repeatedly warned by their
Superiors or spiritual directors that their conscience is too lax and that they should not trust
their own judgment in matters of religious obli-

gations, but rather rely upon the advice and suggestions of God's representatives—only such ailing and partially blinded souls are in danger of missing God's Will and good pleasure because they disregard such warnings and continue to rely upon their own opinion and judgment.

Yes, Dear Soul, there is no other way to attain close union with God and consequently to enjoy real and sweet happiness in the service of God, than wholehearted love for God's Will and good pleasure, both in great and in seemingly unimportant matters. Let, then, the Holy Will of God be your supreme and only ideal, in theory and in practice.

4

RELUCTANT SURRENDER
TO GOD'S DECREES

Let us turn away our mind from those miserable creatures in Hell who by their own choice and fault are living in a state of revolt against their Maker. They cannot escape God's eternal decrees, God's Will, that punishes them according to the requirements of Divine Infinite Justice. But they refuse to surrender and to acknowledge the righteousness of their punishments. They do not deserve our compassion, on account of the obstinate malice of their will.

When saying: "Reluctant surrender" in the present discussion, we mean deliberate acquiescence in the Will of God, though with mixed feelings, with inner sadness and voluntary bitterness. The vast majority of people on earth, Christians not excepted, preserve this attitude toward the Will of God. They refrain from open revolt against Divine Omnipotence, from sinful murmurings against God too, since they know all this would be useless anyhow. As reasonable and enlightened people they see and feel only

17

too well their weakness and nothingness.

Are such spiritual dispositions of any value for the soul's salvation? Undoubtedly, they are. God, in His infinite goodness, deigns to recognize every spark of good will on our part. And any kind of surrender to God's decrees, imperfect as the motives may be, means good will. Such elementary surrender, if it continues for many years and in varying circumstances, hints at solid Christian virtue, and eventually may assume characteristics of genuine perfection. Unfortunately, those surrendering themselves unconditionally to God, without any exception whatsoever, are not the average type of Christians. We meet too seldom such "true Israelites," even among sincere worshippers of God.

Reluctant surrender to the Will of God is more a result of fear than the outflow of love for God. Now, apart from genuine, childlike love of God, it is very hard to persevere in the practice of great virtue, such as unreservedly embracing God's Will in whatever form it may manifest itself. Acting through servile fear, the service of God gradually becomes tedious, and it takes almost a miracle of Divine grace in such circumstances to keep a soul upon the road to salvation and sanctity. Hence, even ordinary Christians are advised and urged assiduously to foster in their hearts a true love toward their heavenly Father, and to substitute the motive of love for that of fear in God's service.

How much more is a religious soul obliged to acquiesce in the Divine Will out of love! Is not love toward God the only proper atmosphere of the whole religious life? The love of God has chosen and destined a number of souls from eternity to praise and to serve Him in a religious community, to lead an angelic life on earth, and thus merit incomparable glory and happiness in Heaven. Love of God must, therefore, animate every religious in fulfilling its obligations and in complying with the good pleasure of God. For love can be repaid only with love.

Religious souls so frequently read and meditate upon the eternal love of God toward man, and about the reciprocal love we owe our heavenly Father, that it should seem almost impossible for them to leave the sublime path of love and to serve God from a lower motive, or to grow lukewarm in doing His Will. Yet it is always possible that relapse into tepidity or even into bad, if not directly sinful habits, may occur, despite all the incentives to fervor daily presented to religious people. Perseverance upon the road of love is conditioned by strenuous cooperation with the grace of God, and this is neither easy nor comfortable. No wonder, then, that a number of veterans in religion fall back into the primitive state of forced, elementary surrender to God's Will, instead of embracing it with increasing love and tenderness.

How pitiable the fate of these mercenaries in religion. Their fatigue in the service of God is increasing daily, whereas their merit for Heaven diminishes steadily so as to become even doubtful. Some eventually lose their vocation, and lead a very unhappy existence in the world, haunted incessantly by the remembrance of the inestimable favors received from God, and never forgetting their own black ingratitude. It is to be feared that some may even definitely draw away from God and forfeit their eternal salvation.

"Reluctant surrender" to the Will of God admits, however, a different meaning which has nothing to do with deliberate resistance to God's Will. A case in point would be that of a very fervent religious who, deprived for a time of all spiritual sweetness, finds it difficult to submit to God's decrees, and only does so by great and continued spiritual exertion. He must force himself, his nature, his feelings, to acquiesce in the Will of God. What is the value of this self-imposed and forced acquiescence before God? Undoubtedly, it is of greater merit for Heaven than all those acts of virtue that are accomplished easily and naturally. The more it costs the soul to comply with God's good pleasure, the stronger her love for God.

Did not Our Lord Himself strongly exert His human will to acquiesce in the Will of His heavenly Father as to His imminent Passion and death? And yet, the love of the Saviour for His Father and His good pleasure was beyond every human conception.

The simple prayer "Thy Will be done" may have many and various meanings, from a mere and reluctant submission to God's omnipotence unto a childlike or even seraphic love of God's good pleasure in all details of life. Hence, it is an expression of either elementary good will and a basic desire for salvation, or of superhuman sanctity and union with God. It all depends upon the inner dispositions of the devout soul, upon the degree of her love toward God, and upon the firmness of her determination to comply with all the wishes of the Divine Heart.

It is then correct to say that sanctity consists in the union of our will with the Will of God. However, this general definition encompasses innumerable kinds and degrees of sanctity. Consequently, it would be a mistake to believe that our sanctification is complete on account of the fact that we never openly and consciously revolt against the Will of our heavenly Father. Such an assumption is warranted only in as far as it takes the term "sanctity" in a general sense, that of being in God's grace and in good relationship with Him.

And yet, those souls may rejoice and be glad who have achieved that initial and basic victory of unconditionally subordinating their will, though only in absolutely essential matters, to the Law and Will of God. They have definitely taken the first step upon the only and infallible road leading to real and lasting happiness. Even very imperfect Christians who at times yield to violent temptations and offend God grievously, but who are always anxious to restore their former good relationship with God, or who sincerely and steadily try to unite their will with the Will of God, feel incomparably more content and happy in life than all those obstinate sinners who live as if they were quite independent of their Maker. Obstinate sinners resemble the evil spirits in Hell, and share the mortal torments of those revolted angels.

What powerful incentive for every soul, whether in or out of the convent, to strive assiduously after a more perfect union with God's good pleasure. Such union is an inexhaustible source of inner peace, of genuine joy and supernatural bliss! On the other hand, they do themselves irreparable harm who make themselves believe that happiness can be found in life, insisting upon independence of the Divine Will and Law! They walk, as the Holy Ghost puts it, in darkness and in the shadow of death.

5

HESITANT, APPREHENSIVE ATTITUDE TOWARD THE WILL OF GOD

The average pious Christian shows himself as it were diffident in the face of possible trials that God may send or allow to come upon him. He is fearful of his Father in Heaven on account of His infinite power, justice and sanctity. And when the trials set in, his soul falls into a state of confusion, for he neither accepts God's Will wholeheartedly, nor dares to revolt against it. His attitude changes from moment to moment, a curious mixture of good intentions and spiritual weakness.

Lukewarm religious people at times resemble such irresolute servants of God. At moments, when their fervor is strengthened by pious meditations, spiritual reading or the living word of God, they feel encouraged to offer themselves in prayer as victims, willing to toil, to suffer and to die for God's glory and love. And in fact, should a trial come upon them at such a time, they probably would readily comply with God's good pleasure. However, their virtue not yet being firmly established and rooted, they will suffer frequent setbacks when the Will of God seems rather difficult and they are less favorably disposed.

To estimate the degree of perfection in these souls, it must be ascertained whether their hesitance to do Divine Will is diminishing and their courage increasing, or whether the very opposite is true. If their victories are many in combatting their weak and cowardly nature, then the sporadic small defeats are rather unimportant. They may be accounted as valiant and fervent souls and their eventual sanctification seems to be assured. But a growing hesitance to accept crosses is indicative of tepidity which may easily lead to sins and to estrangement from God.

In the realm of the spiritual life, there is neither an easy nor a comfortable road. One goes either upward closer to the ideals of sanctity, or downwards to naturalism, ugly sensualism and sinful passions. That is the meaning of the maxim contained in Holy Scripture that human life is and must be a spiritual combat. Human nature, infected by the poison of Original Sin, doggedly adheres and will ever adhere to its alleged right to unlimited freedom, whereas God can never forego His eternal prerogatives as the Maker of man. So peace can be established between the human soul and God only on the basis of unconditional and willing surrender on the part of man.

It must however be clearly stated that there can be no wrong in a hesitancy in the service of God which is inherent in human nature and never can be radically conquered. It implies rather fear than a wavering or reluctant will. The most outstanding example of this characteristic of human nature is presented in the person of Our Lord Jesus Christ, preparing for His Passion and death in the Garden of Olives. On account of the external appearances the Apostles could have had the impression that Jesus only reluctantly complied with the eternal Will of His Father, whereas in fact, not even a shadow of opposition against the Divine Will was possible in the most holy soul of Jesus, true man and true God.

The human nature of Jesus was overwhelmed with immeasurable anguish at the vision of forthcoming events. His soul shuddered at the sight of the most cruel torments and of the infamous death on Calvary, as any man on earth would shudder in similar circumstances. However, in contradistinction to those who oppose the Divine decrees, Jesus not only submitted to the Will of His Father, but He embraced it with infinite love.

To a certain degree, souls sincerely abandoned to God and to His good pleasure may recognize a "double law" in their nature and heart. Nature may violently oppose God's Will, while the heart and the will of the saintly soul firmly determine to adhere to the Divine Will. Hence there may be a natural reluctance to accept trials, but there is no real hesitancy in complying with God's good pleasure.

As a soul advances in perfection, in love toward God, its natural cowardice in the face of suffering may gradually diminish. It may almost disappear toward the end of the road to sanctity. On the other hand, however, natural weakness may persist in other instances. Indeed, some saintly persons unquestionably progressing daily in virtue, may realize their natural weakness more distinctly as years go by, and their physical health is impaired. And yet, their union with the Will of God cannot be questioned. They develop a more perfect and closer union with God.

Real hesitancy in doing the Divine Will is probable, if not certain, whenever the following symptoms appear:

First, consider the soul confronted with suffering, demanding inevitable sacrifice, which consciously protests against the trial which it knows, at least confusedly, is coming from God or is permitted by God. The opposition may last only for moments so as to resemble a mere temptation, and complete surrender may follow soon. Before God, however, an infidelity has been committed, because the soul did not comply with God's good pleasure immediately. The shortest moment of conscious opposition against the

Divine Will is tantamount to moral imperfection and guilt.

Secondly, the soul's attitude is imperfect if, when her trial begins, she indulges in sadness and bitter sentiments, while expressing her surrender to God's decrees. She does not wholeheartedly and unreservedly unite herself with the Will of God. Involuntary sadness is no sin or infidelity. It may even increase the soul's merit. To yield, however, to despondency in the face of suffering means some kind of opposition or hesitancy.

Thirdly, there is some hesitance of the human will whenever a suffering soul yields to apprehension that it might not be able to persevere in perfect surrender, owing to insufficient Divine assistance. Such inner sentiments amount to deficient trust in God and His omnipotent grace. A really faithful soul must always be confident and sure that she can achieve everything when relying upon God. Otherwise, she is guilty of pusillanimity.

As long as such and similar imperfections mark our attitude toward the Divine Will, in whatever form it is manifested to us, we have many reasons to humble ourselves before God on account of our selfishness, cowardice and general tepidity. All these weaknesses must be conquered before our soul will be able to enter into a close union with God and enjoy lasting peace and happiness in the service of God.

Those servants of God, however, who can at least be credited with a general and imperfect compliance with all Divine decrees and God's good pleasure, should be very thankful to God for what His grace has accomplished for their sanctification. They are far above the masses of sinful and worldly people who live, as a rule, in a state of continuous opposition to the Will of God. The first worthwhile victories on the road leading to Heaven and sanctity will be followed by further spiritual triumphs, if the soul continues valiantly to cooperate with the grace of God.

Doubtless, it will take time, perhaps many years, to ascend to higher levels of union with the Will of God, and to higher degrees of sanctity, which is in fact one and the same thing. Though that spiritual striving and combat may be thornful and toilsome, it will increase the happiness of the soul. And when final victory is achieved, the valiant soul will be in the very vestibule of Heaven.

6

GROWING DETERMINATION IN COMPLYING WITH THE WILL OF GOD

Feelings and sentiments form an integral part of our human nature and play an important role in our sanctification. Natural dispositions, inclinations, passions, may either slow down our spiritual progress, even endanger our salvation, or effectively help us in the spiritual combat. Consequently, the role of sentiments must not be underestimated, nor should it be exaggerated. They are, after all, only a secondary factor in the realm of spirituality.

Firm adherence to the Will of God is the principal proof of real perfection and sanctity. The firmer that adherence, the higher the soul's sanctity. Hence, it is of special interest for those bound to perfection that they know how to estimate the degrees of firmness in adhering to Divine Will. Mistakes in this field are only too common.

Most people striving for perfection are wont to appraise the firmness of their will by the sensible fervor they feel at the moment of prayer

when good resolutions are made. If their heart
is filled with sublime sentiments and unusual
ardor, they are prone to believe that their resolutions will prove unshakable. On the other hand,
whenever a pious soul feels rather languid and
indifferent, she is discouraged because of her apparent hesitance to accept God's Will, although
she sincerely and assiduously exerts herself to
comply with the Divine Will.

Meanwhile, sensible ardor and eagerness prove
to be very unreliable symptoms of moral firmness. Man's passions are fickle and changeable
as are also his pious sentiments, unless supported
and strengthened by some superior power. How
often people seemingly burning with seraphic
love of God at the time of prayer and meditation, yield to temptations of selfishness, anger
and pride, but a few hours later! Obviously, their
love was not so perfect as it seemed to be and
their adherence to the good pleasure of God is
rather theoretical. They can be credited with be-
ginnings of good will and virtue, but hardly with
established perfection. They lack that firm character which is essential to real sanctity.

On the other hand, a soul naturally inclined
to despondency and generally deprived of pious
and ardent feelings, if assisted by abundant Divine grace, may yet be in possession of a very
strong will and unshakably adhere to the Will
of God.

Consequently, it is not advisable to exert one-self immoderately to stir up religious, pious sentiments. Undboubtedly, our whole being belongs to God and we are obliged to love Him with our whole heart and strength, which includes our feelings, too. But since feelings and sentiments cannot be produced at will, and since religious sentiments more particularly depend upon the kind of graces each soul receives from God, it is of no avail to elicit by force such spiritual feelings, because they should be spontaneous. Besides, our relation to God is entirely dependent upon the disposition of our will. This will is the noblest faculty of our nature and its acts cannot be compared with merely sensible feelings.

In the light of these theological and psychological principles, it is easy to realize that the perfection of our adherence to God's Will cannot be measured by the intensity of sentiments which accompany our good resolutions. Consequently, sweet and sensible feelings constitute but an accidental, probable evidence of our good will and our moral perfection. The decisive factor is always the soul's determination to comply and to unite itself closer and closer with the Holy Will of God. Again, this determination, its firmness and perfection, asserts itself not so much by certain sensible affections and emotions as by perseverance and holy stubbornness in keeping the promises made to God.

Yes, the strength of our will and of its adherence to God's good pleasure should be estimated by the degree of our perseverance in either keeping our resolutions or returning to them again and again, hundreds and thousands of times, after a temporary defeat. A valiant soul can certainly be credited with a very firm will and a very faithful adherence to the Divine Will, which implies a high degree of sanctity, if only she shows holy stubbornness in renewing again and again the spiritual combat against her human weakness. The number of her defeats is of no special importance.

The determination of a soul to comply with God's Will at any cost is evidenced, in a certain sense, with greater clarity, rather by the repeated efforts made after failure than by a series of easy victories. For, it takes a kind of heroism to begin over again and again when striving for sanctity, despite countless defeats. One has, then, to hope against hope, which is indeed a superhuman virtue.

A little explanation, however, must be made here. The term "defeat" as used in this discussion is not to be taken in the sense of deliberate faults, especially grievous faults. It is unthinkable that a soul sincerely abandoned to God, despite assiduous endeavors to unite her will with God's Will, should often relapse into grievous sin, or into entirely deliberate venial sins. Only semi-voluntary faults and general weakness of a soul can coexist with sincere abandonment to God and with faithful adherence to His Holy Will.

Our determination to conform with God's good pleasure should not be regarded as a particular virtue, but rather as a symptom and measure of our general perfection and sanctity. For, sanctity consists essentially in the love of God, in conformity with God's good pleasure, according to the unanimous teachings of all Saints and all theologians. Hence, no real progress in adherence to the Divine Will can be achieved unless all Christian virtues, above all the theological virtue of charity, are assiduously and intensely cultivated. But on the other hand, the least advance in solid and tender devotion to the Will of God is indicative of actual progress in the general field of evangelical perfection.

Without childlike love for the Will of God, our work of sanctification is paralyzed. All other virtues, sublime and attractive as they may seem, are of very restricted value before God, if they are not related to God's Will and good pleasure. Such virtues bear the character of sheer natural qualities. As God Himself is the Beginning and the End of all things, so His adorable Will and good pleasure must be the ultimate motive of all Christian virtues.

The initial stages of our union with the Will

of God, as a rule, are characterized by toilsome spiritual efforts connected often with bitter moral sufferings. The soul's love toward God has not yet reached such a high degree as to sweeten the spiritual combat. Gradually, however, the yoke of Christ becomes lighter and compliance with the Divine Will is followed by more spiritual consolations. Ultimately, doing God's Will as it is recognized from moment to moment seems almost natural and easy to the faithful soul. Her virtue and perfection surely rest upon firm foundations.

Be sure, Dear Soul, that the union of your will with God's Will constitutes a real spiritual treasure, that it resembles that mystic pearl mentioned by Our Lord which is worth buying, even at the highest price. Try, then, to find this Divine gem, and your spiritual life will soon take a new course that leads directly to God, to sweet inner peace, to such happiness as can never be found in creatures. You will not regret the sacrifices offered to God upon this royal way of perfection and sanctity.

7

SUPERNATURAL PEACE, THE SWEET REWARD FOR SUBMITTING TO THE WILL OF GOD

Any opposition to God results in unrest, affliction of spirit and unhappiness. There is no peace for souls who disregard the good pleasure of God. And the more deliberate their opposition or revolt, the more excruciating their moral suffering.

On the contrary, supernatural, heavenly peace descends upon souls abandoned to God, both in theory and in practice. God is Peace infinite and eternal. Hence, those united to Him and to His Holy Will find their souls filled with heavenly peace. Is not this a superabundant reward for all the acts of self-denial which are inevitable upon the way of perfection or total submission to the Will of God?

Obviously, no one can expect perfect peace the very moment he puts foot upon the road of surrender to the Divine Will. It is but gradually that a fervent soul approaches the sublime summits of an undisturbed mystical rest in God.

Probably for years her peace will prove rather uncertain and imperfect, too dependent upon exterior circumstances. However, even this initial and partial peace is a real treasure on earth, incomparably more conducive to real happiness than all merely human and natural gratifications. A tiny bit of peace Divine exceeds in value huge mountains of doubtful earthly pleasures. For, supernatural peace constitutes the very core of our happiness, both on earth and in eternity.

Peace of soul admits of several meanings. There are certain kinds of peace which we are called upon to sacrifice on the altar of Divine love, as we are expected to renounce earthly things, not essential to our true happiness. This applies particularly to that spiritual sweetness which we enjoy at times in the service of God and which gives us a slight foretaste of Heaven. It is that sensible peace which, as a rule, proves rather fickle and unreliable. Even saints and souls perfectly abandoned to God are often deprived of this kind of peace. It is well to remember that Our Lord Jesus Christ Himself was willing to suffer and to die on Calvary in an atmosphere of affliction and bitterness, totally opposed to all sensible sweetness, to all consolation.

Our senses may suffer so intensely at times, as to make us feel that we have lost supernatural peace, the very core of happiness. But this is not true, so long as we endeavor to unite our-

selves with the Holy Will of God, even though
our efforts may seem poor and ineffective. In
the supernatural sense of the term, nothing else
is essential to real peace and happiness, except
the sincere desire and continued effort to comply with the good pleasure of God in everything. Only deliberate opposition to the Divine
Will definitely deprives our soul of supernatural
peace and bliss.

Whatever sacrifices God may impose upon us
on the road to Heaven and sanctity, He will never
demand the sacrifice of that inner, purely
spiritual, truly Divine peace which inevitably
results from our union with God's Will, or even
from our sincere efforts to effect that celestial
union. Solely this spiritual peace constitutes an
essential part of our happiness. The above mentioned sensible peace is only an additional, unnecessary factor. Hence a soul striving for
perfection and following in the footsteps of our
crucified Lord has nothing to fear whilst following the Divine Will. She may suffer at times,
she may pass through a real martyrdom, feeling
herself totally abandoned by God, but the innermost part of her being will always be filled
with real peace. She will never feel unhappy, as
Our Lord never could feel unhappy, though immersed in an ocean of suffering.

Only one thing might warrant apprehension
and uneasiness in the soul, despite its determi-

nation to remain always in perfect accord with
God's good pleasure: this is the remembrance
of human weakness and instability. Who can be
sure that he will remain constant in perfect
submission to the Divine Will? And the more
ardent a soul's love for God, the more she will
suffer at the very thought of possible future
infidelity.

Indeed, if anything on earth is able to disquiet
a soul abandoned to God, it will certainly be
the fear of future infidelities to Divine grace. Thus
when an enlightened soul clearly views her
spiritual misery and realizes her many weaknesses,
will she not be upset and overwhelmed by
despondency?

And yet, souls faithful to grace and relying
upon grace manage, as a rule, to preserve their
inner peace, despite clear consciousness of their
own helplessness in matters of their salvation
and sanctification. How do they achieve this goal?
In a very simple manner: By deepening and perfecting their childlike confidence in God.

Confidence in God seemingly does not give
perfect assurance of perseverance and, consequently, is not able to rid the soul of all apprehension concerning our future spiritual welfare.

In fact, it is true that no soul on earth can
have absolute assurance as to her future fidelity
to Divine grace and to perseverance in the service of God, and she has even less assurance as

to her perseverance upon the way of perfection. But childlike confidence in God can reach so high a degree of perfection that the soul feels practically certain of perseverance. It is the Holy Ghost Himself who establishes that moral certitude in a faithful soul and preserves her from all disquietude. After all, then, solid inner peace based upon God's grace and mercy can be arrived at by souls who wholeheartedly cooperate with grace.

Stable supernatural peace constitutes not only the sweetest reward on earth for willing submission to the Will of God, but it may very effectively further our sanctification. In an atmosphere of peace God's grace can operate almost unopposed within our soul; and on the other hand, our mind is able to penetrate much deeper into all mysteries of the spiritual life than is possible in the midst of many worries and troubles. That is why supernatural peace is praised by all masters of spirituality as one of the most precious gifts of God.

Since for every real good the proportionate price must be paid, so the Divine peace can be won only through continued and assiduous exertion, through many acts of self-denial and sacrifices offered to God. An easy-going life will never be a peaceful life, in the supernatural sense. The old adage *"Si vis pacem, para bellum"*—who wants peace must prepare for war—applies to the spiritual life even more exactly than to nations. But once a soul has definitely prepared for armed peace, and has achieved a series of major victories, she will find the inevitable spiritual combat not only easier but, in a certain sense, very interesting and attractive, as any form of fight or game is interesting.

The most difficult aspect of submission to the Divine Will is that of humble surrender to all legitimate representatives of God, regardless of their virtues. But a soul unfaithful in meeting the obligations of holy obedience deludes herself if she makes herself believe that she is loving God's Will nonetheless. At best, she can be credited with some good will, with a vague desire to do the Will of God. However, since her good will is not sincere enough, and rather theoretical than real, she cannot enjoy the Divine peace promised to those lovingly united with the Will of God.

Let us be valiant and resolute in complying with God's Holy Will and good pleasure.

CAN WE IN ALL CIRCUMSTANCES ASCERTAIN THE REAL WILL OF GOD?

Most Christians believe we cannot. At any rate, not always and everywhere. Many religious striving for perfection share that opinion.

Meanwhile, if God insists upon our compliance with His Sacred Will, which no reasonable creature can doubt, how could He deprive us of the necessary means to recognize His real good pleasure in all circumstances of life? Should He leave us in the dark as to His Will, He would—so to say—contradict Himself, which is an absurd assumption. Enlightened and saintly souls were always convinced that all those sincerely desirous of doing God's Will are at all times, under all circumstances, in a position to realize what God wants them to do. Are they right, or is God's good pleasure really doubtful in certain circumstances? This problem must be discussed thoroughly and clearly answered if our sanctification is to be secured.

The most important distinction to be made here is between the real, objective Will of God and the supposed or assumed Will of God. The supposed or assumed Divine Will or good pleasure means the Will of God as man views it and is able to recognize it in every particular case; whereas the objective Will of God is independent of what we recognize or assume. Obviously enough, the objective and the assumed, or subjective Will of God, may prove quite different in many instances, because our mind is so fallible, and the Divine Will, as it exists in itself, is not directly accessible to any created intelligence. Only in certain substantial matters revealed by God Himself or defined by His infallible Church can we obtain absolute certitude as to the objective Will of God. We are—for instance—absolutely sure that God wants all men to be saved, that He infinitely detests moral evil or sin, that He insists upon our loving Him with our whole heart.

In our practical daily life we must assume that certain acts are conformable with God's good pleasure and Will, though often we cannot rid our mind of doubts concerning the particular case. To suspend our action until we reach complete certitude as to the objective Will of God in every instance would make the service of God an unbearable burden. So what is the inference? Are we obliged to act at the risk of opposing the good pleasure of God, so as to displease Him or even to commit a sin against His infinite

Majesty? If this were true, then human life would become a real torment for all those who love God with childlike affection and sincerely try to sanctify themselves.

Fortunately enough, the situation is not so dark in our relationship to the Divine Will. For, the only condition of pleasing God and of sanctifying one's soul is our sincere compliance with God's good pleasure in as far as we are able to recognize it. Nothing more is required for our salvation and for the highest degree of sanctity. Consequently, our human fallibility constitutes no real obstacle to spiritual progress, not even to heroic perfection. In other words, a soul of good will may be daily mistaken in many cases as to the objective Will of God. She may act, indeed, against the real good pleasure of God. If only she persistently exerts herself to find out God's Will, and applies the necessary means to attain this goal, she must be called a good servant of God. She is undoubtedly upon the road leading to sanctity. For, only deliberate opposition to the Will of God is morally evil and blocks our sanctification. Mistakes which cannot be avoided are morally indifferent.

Let us stress, however, this little condition: Mistakes which cannot be avoided. . .invincible errors, as they are termed in theology.

Many mistakes actually can be avoided, if a soul is sincerely looking for information and enlightenment, if she consistently follows the way of humble deference to all representatives of God, if she tries to strive for perfection under spiritual direction, and above all, if she is very faithful in prayer. Obviously, these conditions are not easily fulfilled. It takes earnest and continued exertion to remain steadfast upon the way of humility, obedience and submission to all legitimate superiors and spiritual guides. And it is only too easy to make ourselves believe that our view of the Divine Will is right and that of our superiors and directors, wrong. And whenever a soul yields to such temptations and acts independently, ignoring the instructions, suggestions and orders of God's representatives, then her mistakes in matters pertaining to the Divine Will are no longer harmless. She is mistaken through her own fault, in consequence of her pride and her spirit of independence.

On the other hand, however, some mistakes made in exploring the Will of God can hardly be avoided. The instructions obtained from superiors or spiritual directors cannot be so detailed as to preclude every practical doubt. We are obliged at times to decide by ourselves what the true good pleasure of God is in a concrete case. Should we then misunderstand the real Will of God and act according to this error, our mistake would entail no evil consequences for our soul. God, infinitely good and just, never takes amiss the soul's invincible error. And an error is indeed invincible, when no doubt occurs in our mind as to the righteousness of our behavior or when we are not in a position to obtain more accurate information about the good pleasure of God.

Hence, every soul of good will is sufficiently able to ascertain, at any time and in all circumstances, what God wants her to do in particular cases. It all depends, however, upon her really good will. The general good intention, as it is repeated even by very imperfect, unfaithful and partially blinded souls, certainly does not guarantee a real accord of our will with the Will of God. There is too much danger of semivoluntary self-deception, as to what is or is not conformable with God's good pleasure. But those souls show a genuine good will, who remain humbly submissive to their superiors and spiritual directors, accepting and acting on their decisions and wishes, instead of following their own personal opinion.

Persons afflicted with a fearful, scrupulous conscience may very often have difficulties and doubts concerning the real Will of God. They may feel unable, as a rule, to make up their mind as to what is God's Will under certain circumstances. But even these afflicted souls are never deprived of the necessary supernatural light to discover the real good pleasure of God. This light

is ordinarily granted them by means of holy obedience. If only they unhesitatingly adhere to the
injunctions of their superiors and spiritual guides,
if they disregard their doubts according to the
advice of the representatives of God, to choose
in practice what they believe corresponds better
to holy obedience, they will be in perfect accord
with God's good pleasure, multiple and excruciating as their worries and doubts may be.

No one, therefore, should excuse himself from
doing God's Will under the pretext of being unable to recognize the real good pleasure of God.
It is certain that God never permits a soul to
be placed in a position where she is forced to
commit a sin. It is just as certain that every soul
sincerely exerting herself to comply with God's
good pleasure is able to recognize the Holy Will
of God either directly or through holy obedience
in all possible circumstances.

9

THE WILL OF GOD
IN OUR DAILY WORK

Every reasonable man will readily agree with
the principle that work is everybody's duty on
earth according to the eternal designs of our
Maker. To decide, however, what particular work
each individual should perform to comply perfectly with the good pleasure of God is a more
complex problem. Various sorts of labor are of
different value, and prove to be more or less conducive to the glory of God, to man's salvation
and to his general spiritual welfare. Meanwhile,
we can fully enjoy our work only after making
sure that it is, indeed, the kind of work and
profession God wants us to perform under the
circumstances.

But has God provided us with sufficient means
to select safely among many possible professions
just that kind of work which best corresponds
to the eternal designs of God, in reference to
our earthly and future happiness? We can be sure,
because of God's infinite Wisdom and Goodness, that our loving heavenly Father has not

47

withheld from us the means necessary to recognize His Holy Will or good pleasure.

In reference to the Will of God, mankind can be divided into two quite different groups. The vast human masses are entitled to enjoy, unreservedly, their natural, personal freedom in daily life, provided they comply with the basic Law of God as expressed in the Ten Commandments, and in human laws, ecclesiastical or secular, which explain and apply the general law to particular circumstances and cases. Another group, very small in number, but called up to perform the more important tasks in human society, voluntarily renounces its personal freedom through the vow of obedience in the religious life, to do God's Will more safely and perfectly.

Ordinary Christians generally are of the opinion that it does not matter at all before God what profession they choose, if only it can be practiced within the limits of the Ten Commandments. Are they right? The answer can be: Yes and no. It will be "yes" whenever a number of professions are considered which are equally conducive to God's glory and to the salvation of the individual involved. It must be a hesitant "yes" if not a definite "no" in instances where the profession makes a soul's salvation hazardous or hardly contributes in any way whatsoever to the glory of God. For, no one has the right deliberately to endanger his salvation, and everybody is bound in conscience to live and to act above all for the glory of his Creator, at least through a general virtual good intention.

It is to be regretted that most people choose their profession, and decide in daily practice to act without regard to the amount of glory their life and their particular actions will bring to God. At best, they try to remain within the limits of the Ten Commandments, and make themselves believe this is all God expects them to do. Man is created to praise and to love his Maker with his whole mind and his whole heart, that is to say, he should exert himself to give God more and more glory. He is not necessarily expected to lead a life of heroic perfection. But with moderate care, without taking upon himself an unbearable burden, man is certainly able to render great glory and love to his Maker. He does harm to himself if he disregards this eternal Will of God.

Since men generally are spiritually lukewarm in their service of God, it behooves religious to live more in accord with the Will of God. That is the best way to atone before God for the black ingratitude of millions of thoughtless and negligent people.

The moral perfection religious souls are bound to practice according to their holy vows implies assiduous efforts to refer all parts and all moments of work to God, directly and actually, as far as possible with the grace of God. The virtual, subconscious good intention, though sufficient to secure some merit before God, should by no means diminish our striving for a more perfect, more actual intention. Doubtless, our spiritual progress is dependent, to a great extent, upon our spiritual dispositions during our work, since so many hours are devoted daily to external activity.

The simplest method of sanctifying our daily work consists, according to the unanimous teaching of spiritual masters and theologians, in regarding each duty of our daily life as God's Will, and consequently, in performing it not only with the necessary exactness but with cheerful willingness and love. For, to love the Will of God is tantamount to love of God Himself, and to real sanctity.

However, too many religious are tempted to doubt whether a certain duty, imposed upon them by obedience, should be regarded as the Divine Will. How can this work forced upon me by my superiors be God's Will? It is excessive work. It interferes with my spiritual life. The superiors should take account of my special abilities for certain labors, instead of ignoring my natural aptitude. The whole plan is imprudent. Various occupations are not justly distributed. Why must I always be the scapegoat to perform the most unpleasant and the hardest work?...No! All this cannot possibly agree with the Will of God. It is obviously a result of my superior's self-will...

Is not this, in many instances, the reasoning of religious bored with certain kinds of unpleasant work? And if they yield to such temptations, what will be the value of their daily toil before God? One may fear that work done with such spiritual dispositions is more like a series of infidelities than it is meritorious for Heaven.

Beware then, Dear Soul, of the many snares prepared for you by your selfish nature. Never forget the principles laid down by the Saints about the Will of God, in reference to your life in general, and particularly in matters connected with your daily occupations. No doubt, your superiors may be mistaken in some cases. They may act imprudently. Before God they may be guilty of injustice or lack of charity. And many other charges can be launched against your superiors, in the light and spirit of purely human justice and wisdom. But all these objections, warranted as they may seem, are not able to nullify the truth that the will of your superiors is for you the expression of the Divine Will.

This principle admits of a few exceptions which are clearly indicated in your religious rule or in the ecclesiastical and regular law. You are not obliged to continued superhuman exertion in your work, even though some superiors, disregarding your difficulties, insist upon more and greater efforts on your part. You are perfectly obedient, if you do what is humanly possible. You cannot, however, be credited with sufficient obedience if your standard in life is a comfortable existence, with little regard to the needs of your institute and to the wishes of God's representatives. Besides, you are entitled to appeal to higher authorities if you are convinced in conscience that in your particular community, external work is insisted upon to such an extent as to preclude all care of the proper spiritual life. For, your right to lead a truly religious life cannot be questioned. But until a decision is obtained from higher superiors, you are expected to comply with the demands of your local superiors. In fine, whenever you feel and see that your working conditions are certainly abnormal, not consistent with true glory of God and with your spiritual welfare, or with your unquestionable personal rights, you may place your case before the higher superiors. They then are bound to change or improve the existing conditions. But this should always be done in the spirit of holy indifference as to the final result. In the meantime, the Will of God for you is to follow the regulations of your immediate superiors.

In the present generation, in this century of prevailing "super-activism," the working conditions in religious communities are only too often abnormal. Complaints about being overtaxed with work can be heard everywhere. Nowadays it takes a very strong character and very abundant grace of God to care adequately for one's sanctification, because of this inevitable overburdening with external occupations.

You may, however, be consoled and comforted by this thought: If you are overtaxed with work without your fault, if you are not able to change the abnormal conditions of your daily labors, and if you accept your hard work as coming directly from the hands of God, if that work means nothing but the Will of God to you, and if you exert yourself to love it wholeheartedly, then you can suffer no harm in your spiritual life. Your work will be tantamount to prayer, even to very perfect, incessant, contemplative prayer. And this kind of prayer always leads to rapid and great sanctification.

In short, to love God's Will in your daily work, to unite with God during that work, is a very simple but infallible means to please God, to attain the highest perfection, and even to enjoy a bit of heavenly bliss here on earth.

Let this then be your firm resolution: To see God's Will in every bit of your daily work, tedious and hard though it may be, and to love this Divine Will as you love God Himself. As long as you meet this condition, you have no reason to worry about your sanctification and your glory in eternity. You are upon the royal road to sanctity.

10

THE WILL OF GOD IN DAILY DIFFICULTIES AND FAILURES

Success in all undertakings is commonly regarded as evidence of God's good pleasure in our life and work. On the contrary, frequent failures in our strivings and endeavors seem to hint at discontent on the part of God. But here again the old adage applies: Divine judgments are not human judgments.

Was not Our Lord's earthly life one apparent failure? He came to redeem humanity, to lay foundations of the Kingdom of God on earth, and to draw all of mankind to the feet of His Heavenly Father. Now, His career and life came to an abrupt end on Calvary, at the age of 33, by the most disgraceful death on the Cross, as a result of the hatred and rivalry of His enemies...humanly speaking, the most appalling disaster our mind can imagine. And yet, this apparent "failure" and tragedy constitute the ineffable mystery of our Redemption. This is the cause and the source of all our joy and happiness, in time and in eternity.

How encouraging is the whole life of Our Redeemer to those often deprived of success in their life and activity, as a result of countless difficulties that block their way and frustrate their best intentions! True, it is not easy to view things from a supernatural and Divine angle. But souls faithful to prayer always are granted abundant light from Heaven to adjust their thoughts and feelings to the eternal designs of Divine Wisdom and Love. Those neglecting prayer are themselves at fault that they cannot rise to a supernatural viewpoint.

In the biographies of saintly souls we read that they sincerely regarded difficulties and failures in performing their duties as tokens of God's good pleasure. They were thankful to God for His blessings; yet sufferings and humiliations accompanying their works and strivings were accepted and welcomed by the Saints as the most precious gifts of the Heavenly Father. Enlightened and saintly souls feel uneasy unless their undertakings and works are marked by the sign of the Cross, that is to say, by difficulties and sufferings.

No doubt, God wishes us to accept hardships, obstacles, failures and humiliations in our professional work and in our whole life. Thus we increase our merits and avoid in our souls that proud and self-confident feeling as if we of ourselves had achieved great results for God's glory

or for the welfare of our neighbors. In the midst
of countless difficulties our soul must preserve
a humble and childlike attitude toward God, the
only source of consolation and strength for
human weakness and nothingness. Continued
success as a rule proves dangerous, if not fatal,
in a supernatural sense, to human nature. As a
result, people too often forget about God, draw
away from His Fatherly Heart, and endanger their
salvation. Do you not see, then, that difficulties
and failures can be real blessings from God?

Total failure of an enterprise may arouse sus-
picion that God's blessing was denied to it from
the beginning. Similarly, too many difficulties
in our work, particularly if they continue for
a long period and make the outlook seem entirely hopeless, may be indicative, too, of Divine displeasure. In such circumstances holy
prudence will suggest a careful examination of
the whole problem, to find out what the real
Will of God may be. For, it would be foolish
self-confidence to maintain that our difficulties
and failures are always unquestionable evidence
of God's blessing and good pleasure. It all depends upon the circumstances and upon our
spiritual dispositions during our work.

Suppose you are working in strict accordance
with holy obedience, and nevertheless serious
obstacles emerge again and again, so as to make
the final success very doubtful. Have you rea-

sons to worry then about the source of your difficulties? Could they be indicative of God's displeasure? By no means! Undoubtedly, you are in accord with the Divine Will, and God certainly is pleased with your endeavors. He sends or permits obstacles to make your work more meritorious. Should continued and increasing difficulties eventually make it evident that God has withdrawn His blessing from the work imposed upon you by obedience, perhaps to warn your superiors that their plans and wishes are not entirely conformable with His Will and designs, you need not worry. For, as far as you and your conscience are concerned, you are undoubtedly doing the Will of God.

The same can be said about your merit and God's good pleasure in your work when performed not under obedience but freely, according to your own decision—provided you meet one essential condition. You must do what you sincerely believe to be in the best accord with God's good pleasure. Then also you are doing the Will of God, although you may partially misunderstand the wishes of the Divine Heart. Difficulties that hamper your activity at times must be readily accepted as trials and as God's Will. They will increase your merits and very effectively further your sanctification.

Under different circumstances, however, difficulties and failures may constitute a warning from God that something is wrong either about the work itself or in your purpose and intention. It is time, then, to examine your conscience and to find out what may displease God in your activity. In such cases you will probably feel uneasy at times about your relationship to the Divine Will.

Let us cite a striking example. Suppose you have asked and obtained from your superiors the approval of some new apostolic work, educational, charitable or directly related to the salvation of souls, and you have some inner uneasiness and incertitude as to the real Will of God. Your conscience warns you that you are shifting for some time, from a life of intense prayer to nervous activity, against the spirit of your religious rule. In this instance, it seems probable that you are following not so much Divine inspiration as your natural inclination for work, for continued activity and for human applause. If, under these circumstances, other indications arise which imply that God does not approve of your excessive work—if the work itself becomes harder and harder, while your spiritual life suffers—would it be prudent to make yourself believe that your difficulties are but trials sent by God? We wonder. . .

In this case, all circumstances rather hint at the fact of the Divine displeasure. There was, probably, some self-will in assuming such additional work, though with the reluctant permission of your superiors. And that is the reason why God's blessing is denied your endeavors.

The sooner you realize and acknowledge your mistake, and return to the sure and royal road of perfect obedience and intense spiritual life, the better for you and for the welfare of souls which you intend to draw to God.

Yes, difficulties and obstacles can and should be regarded as trials coming from God and as evidence of His blessing, but always under this essential condition: If you are living and acting under religious obedience that imposes an unsolicited work upon you, then, undoubtedly, you should disregard all obstacles and look upon them as Divine trials. If you are not a religious and you must make the decision regarding certain good work, then you must have the moral certitude that your activity is in accord with God's good pleasure. If serious doubts occur to your mind as to the Will of God in particular cases, you are advised to consult your spiritual guides and thus you will obtain full certitude as to God's good pleasure.

One thing is certain. Any activity whatsoever that is undertaken for the glory of God and the welfare of souls will inevitably bring with it many difficulties and trials, since it must in a sense be the continuation of Our Lord's life and of His work of Redemption.

11

THE WILL OF GOD
IN OUR SPIRITUAL MISERY

All the material evils of the world cannot distress a soul abandoned to God as much as her own spiritual shortcomings, her human weakness and all the resultant infidelities in the service of God. No human creature, except Jesus and Mary Immaculate, is entirely immune from spiritual misery, in the supernatural sense of the term. And yet, enlightened souls know how to console themselves by accepting that misery as the Will of God—of course, under certain conditions and with important reservations.

First, let us accurately define the conception of spiritual misery.

In a very broad sense, spiritual misery embraces every deliberate sin, both venial and grievous. Sin is the worst and most tragic kind of misery and mishap on earth. But in our discussion we take the word in its restricted sense, namely, as a soul's imperfections and spiritual shortcomings, which are not dependent on her will and consequently constitute no real fault before God. Only this sort of misery which is morally indifferent, neither evil nor good, can be regarded to a certain extent as conformable with the Holy Will of God. For, whatever means real guilt, if only the shadow of guilt, is absolutely opposed to Divine Sanctity and hence to the Will of God.

But spiritual misery is a result of Original Sin and of subsequent personal sins. How, then, can it be called Will of God? Was not man predestined by God to live in a state of innocence, as a perfect child of his Maker, and moreover elevated by sanctifying grace to the inconceivable dignity of a real friend of God—nay, admitted to participate in the very nature of God? No spiritual misery of any kind whatsoever would have afflicted him in that sublime state of innocence. Hence, our spiritual misery seems to be contrary to the eternal Will of God.

Indeed, our present state, our proneness to evil, our countless spiritual shortcomings resulting from sin, were not intended by God from eternity. But following God's prevision of man's sin, God has decided from eternity that the fall of mankind should entail all those consequences which, as a whole, are called our spiritual misery. In other words, there is an immutable law established by God, that sin results in moral weakness, imperfections, revolt of human passions and similiar defects of nature. And this law, obviously, is the Will of God, as it is an inevitable necessity of our condition in the state of fallen nature.

The truth, however, about spiritual misery as the Will of God should not be misunderstood, to the effect that we cease to combat it and absolve ourselves lightheartedly from any responsibility whatever for its symptoms and consequences. This mistake would paralyze our whole spiritual life, perhaps even jeopardize our very salvation. For, the degrees and sorts of spiritual misery are multiple, and while one form of that misery is wholly and certainly innocent before God, another kind may bear characteristics of a doubtful nature, as it can be partially attributed to our fault.

As explained already, our spiritual shortcomings and moral weaknesses are a result not only of Original Sin but of our personal faults as well. The more a soul indulges in sin, the more her general depravity increases and deepens, so as to make her spiritual misery worse. Hence, sinners who deliberately adhere to sinful habits are in a great degree responsible for the weakness of their will at the time of temptations. They should not delude themselves about the grave account to be rendered before God's tribunal, by pointing at the amount of their inborn weakness and misery. For, it is not only inborn and in a certain sense natural, but it is partially due to their own faults and negligence in the service of God.

The line of demarcation between innocent and imputable or sinful spiritual misery often proves rather doubtful and is hard to discover. That is why enlightened and saintly souls are wont to humiliate themselves incessantly, not only for certain sins and infidelities but for their general imperfection and moral weakness as well. They are suspicious that they may be guilty of some negligence in the service of God, so as to be in part responsible for their spiritual misery. Absolute self-confidence as to this point is indicative of pride and spiritual blindness.

Nevertheless, souls whose good will and fervor in the service of God cannot be doubted, especially when they have the assurance of their spiritual guides, should never yield to sadness and worry in spite of their great spiritual misery. They may hopefully rely upon God's mercy, despite all the symptoms of imperfection and human weakness, since their guilt before God is certainly very limited, if there be any at all. God's goodness is infinitely forebearing toward those who show unmistakable good will.

There is no reason for worry on account of involuntary defects and shortcomings, since mere human weakness does not diminish God's glory or cause displeasure to the Divine Heart. On the contrary, inevitable human misery tends to increase the glory of God, as it proves the omnipotence of Divine grace more emphatically and clearly. If a soul endowed with many natural gifts, abilities and virtues is elevated to a high degree of sanctity, it certainly is an evidence of the immense power grace exerts upon her. But when the same thing happens to a soul steeped in spiritual misery, then it appears to be a real miracle of Divine grace. How powerful and effective has the operation of grace proved in Mary Magdalen, Saul of Tarsus and Augustine!

It is true, God, infinitely holy and omniscient, may see traces of personal guilt in what people call sheer human misery. But these semivoluntary faults are easily atoned for by simple acts of contrition and love. And souls established in good will and real abandonment to God are supposed to live permanently in a state of loving contrition. They send up to God countless acts of love and contrition, and that spontaneously, almost without knowing it, and often without using any words whatsoever. So why should they feel despondent at the sight of their spiritual misery?

As a rule, symptoms of human weakness and misery should disappear gradually as a soul abandoned to God is advancing upon the way of perfection and drawing closer to the ideal of union with God. Progressive sanctity is expected to restore, to a certain extent, man's control of his

nature, as it existed in the state of original innocence. However, the ways leading to final sanctification can be very different one from another.
To keep a soul in the state of perfect humility,
God may conceal from her eyes her real progress. He may permit her to be mistaken as to
the extent and gravity of her spiritual misery.
She will feel inclined, then, to view her whole
relationship to God in very dark colors and to
assume that her spiritual misery is rather increasing than diminishing. In such circumstances it
is of extreme importance to rely upon the decisions of our spiritual guides.

But even in the case when the soul's human
weakness is growing, indeed, a soul assiduously
and wholeheartedly striving for religious sanctity should never yield to sadness and despondency. God permits this kind of involuntary
misery for His greater glory.

12

THE WILL OF GOD AMID OUR MORAL SUFFERINGS

The forms and kinds of suffering of the human soul are numberless. They may afflict our nature incomparably more than physical diseases or other external trials, so much so that they cannot be cured by ordinary external remedies. All theologians agree that the moral sufferings of the wicked in Hell immensely surpass the physical torments imposed upon them by Divine Justice.

A permanently afflicted heart signifies an unhappy existence regardless of material abundance, comfort, excellent health, high honors, and plenty of devoted friends. History has recorded many suicides among people who, according to external appearances, should have been the happiest people on earth. Obviously, they were deprived of inner peace, and without peace no real happiness is thinkable.

The term "moral sufferings" is used in this discussion for: sadness, apprehension, despondency, tedious or bitter feelings, remorse of conscience, torturing doubts, temptations, and a general feeling of discontent and unhappiness. In the spiritual life no inner suffering is comparable to the fear of being abandoned by God because of real or imaginary faults. Those subjected to this kind of worry pass through the most cruel martyrdom of the heart. Such a soul endures Purgatory on earth, because she is irresistibly drawn to God, who seemingly turns away from her on account of her sins.

The most painful sufferings of the soul are softened and made tolerable if the person involved is able to believe that her affliction is a trial sent by God. Then sweet inner peace can coexist with a true moral martyrdom. This is evidenced in many lives of saintly souls. This was true of Our Lord Himself, who upon His Cross was apparently abandoned by His Heavenly Father and nonetheless never ceased for a moment to enjoy the sweetest peace in the innermost recesses of His Most Sacred Heart.

Now, the point arises, when and under what conditions can a suffering soul make sure that her trial is the direct or permissive Will of God. Let us thoroughly examine this question.

Some sorts of moral suffering are obviously opposed to God's good pleasure. As long as a sinner adheres to his iniquities without even attempting amendment, and as a result, feels quite unhappy, his moral torments are in no sense con-

formable with the Will of God. It is a self-
inflicted, unnecessary suffering. It cannot be
meritorious for eternity. True, it is God who
sends the remorse of conscience to warn the sinner of his dangerous state and to encourage his
conversion. But after all, the sinner himself is
at fault when God permits remorse to torture
him.

Similarly, a religious soul bound to perfection
may feel utterly discontented in the service of
God; her heart may be filled with bitterness, on
account of her continued and deliberate infidelity in meeting her religious obligations. Is she
entitled to look upon her affliction as a trial sent
by God? By no means! For, she herself is responsible for her dissatisfactory state of mind. She
can at any time rid herself of her suffering by
wholehearted adherence to the Will of God, that
is, by fulfilling her religious obligations. When
she consciously opposes the Holy Spirit by
neglecting her life of prayer and recollection, by
deliberately disregarding her sanctification, then
her aridity and spiritual darkness constitute a
self-inflicted suffering which is of no merit for
eternity.

The vast majority of religious can be classi-
fied as neither strictly perfect nor utterly unfaithful in God's service. Accordingly, they do
not feel entirely satisfied, and are very often
molested by spiritual tediousness and despon-

dency. Their affliction may grow with the years and assume extraordinary proportions. What can we say for the comfort of these imperfect servants of God? Is their affliction God's Will? Is it meritorious for Heaven?

These important questions can be answered only in a general and rather vague manner, because the character and the value of the moral sufferings of imperfect souls depend upon circumstances and conditions. These persons of good will may confidently expect a generous reward from a God infinitely good and merciful, because of their perseverance on the rugged way to perfection, despite the scarcity of celestial consolations. They certainly are entitled to regard their aridities and other spiritual trials as the Divine Will, at least in a restricted sense. They themselves are partially responsible for their persistent afflictions, but they recognize their faults and try to atone for them by renewed endeavors upon the way of true sanctity. Hence, their moral sufferings are not self-inflicted ones, but can be related, at least partially, to the Holy Will of God.

In fine, among the souls sincerely abandoned to God, a certain number belong to the privileged class of sufferers who have no reason at all to doubt that their moral afflictions come from God, to prompt their sanctification, to enhance their resemblance to Jesus Crucified and to augment their merits for Heaven. We mean persons

who can be credited not only with unmistakable, steady fervor in the service of God, but
moreover with assiduous striving for real sanctity. They are resolved at all times and under
all circumstances to do what they believe to be
more conformable with God's good pleasure and
glory, cost what it may. They are tending toward heroism upon the way of perfection. They
consistently follow the outline traced for them
by the representatives of God, by superiors and
spiritual directors, and so avoid all possible self-
deception originating in self-love.

Contrary to a common belief, these saintly
souls are not always immersed in sweet consolation, though their external appearance, peaceful and supernaturally attractive, seems to warrant
such an assumption. We can hardly imagine a
soul more perfectly abandoned to God than the
Little Flower of Lisieux. Divine peace and
heavenly bliss radiated from her innocent countenance, as if her whole life were nothing but
one uninterrupted seraphic smile, originating in
the most perfect love of God. Meanwhile, her
autobiography is evidence of the fact that for
nine long years, from her entering Carmel until
her last breath, Therese was wandering through
a dark tunnel of aridity and apparent abandonment by God. Yes, her whole life was an unin-
terruped act of seraphic love toward God, but
it meant suffering, crucified love, like that of Jesus

when He prayed upon the Cross: My God, why hast Thou forsaken Me? . . .

Not only great Saints but often quite simple souls are called thus to follow in the footsteps of Jesus carrying His Cross to Calvary. They serve God wholeheartedly. They love Him, indeed, above all things in the world, and more than themselves. Day by day, they give unmistakable evidence of their love in the form of generous sacrifices offered to God. And yet, their heart, as a rule, is filled with bitter affliction. It is not that kind of affliction which makes a soul unhappy. No—these true children of God enjoy real heavenly peace. But it is a strictly spiritual peace, deprived of sensible sweetness.

The moral sufferings of these blessed souls are, undoubtedly and manifestly, the Will of God, as were those of Jesus and those of Mary, the Mother of Sorrows. Instead of yielding to despondency, let them sincerely rejoice that they have been worthy of sharing in the Holy Passion of Jesus, until they are united with Jesus in a blissful eternity.

The preceding statements particularly apply to those pious and fervent souls who by God's inscrutable designs are plunged into a state of torturing scrupulosity, or of continuous doubts and apprehensions concerning their relationship to God, their salvation and sanctification. Distressing and painful as their condition may seem, they have nothing to fear or to worry about, if only they follow the rules laid down for them by spiritual masters. Then this grave trial will be rather helpful than harassing on the way of salvation and sanctity.

The rule of rules for all fearful, scrupulous souls is unwavering obedience to the director of conscience—one who is willing to take care of the afflicted penitent, and able to secure true peace to his conscience.

Excessive apprehensiveness in matters of conscience may originate not only from deficient instruction, in a kind of diabolical infestation, but very often it is due to a nervous disorder and cannot be cured easily, if at all curable. But whatever the ultimate source of the affliction, it should be accepted humbly and willingly as God's Will, as the soul's special martyrdom, to speed up her sanctification. It must be emphasized, however, that scrupulosity of any sort can be regarded as the Will of God only insofar as it cannot be controlled and cured by obedience. For, those who refuse to obey their spiritual guides in matters of conscience are at fault themselves if scrupulosity results.

In fact, scrupulosity can always be controlled to some extent, at least, by strict and blind obedience. The feeling of fear may afflict a scrupulous penitent despite his sincere adherence to the given directions. But he can preserve lasting inner peace, provided he ignores all doubts and temptations against obedience. Indeed, he is obliged to ignore these worries, persistent and excruciating as they may be, since it is a positive rule of our holy Faith that every Christian may and must rely upon the directions of his spiritual guides in matters of conscience. According to the same Catholic doctrine, no penitent can commit a sin when he obeys his confessor, even should the latter be mistaken in his judgment.

Here are two rules for those who suffer the martyrdom of scrupolosity: First of all, unhesitant, blind obedience to the director of conscience—and secondly, if apprehensions cannot be stopped and eliminated completely, loving compliance with the Holy Will of God, the painful martrydom of recurring doubts and apprehensions.

13

THE WILL OF GOD IN SICKNESS

Life and health, these are the two supreme natural gifts which human nature covets most, because they are regarded as essential to human happiness. Good health seems even more essential to happiness than life itself, according to purely human reasoning and sentiment. People who can afford it spend whole fortunes to restore their health.

To endure the loss of health for a long period, and perhaps even for a lifetime, requires superhuman virtue, particularly when the disease grows malignant and the pain increases. Thank God, this virtue has been attained by thousands of saintly souls and is practiced even in our day by people who sincerely strive for perfection. Thus it is evidenced again and again that good health is by far less necessary to human well-being on earth than is commonly assumed.

Profound peace of mind and heart may coexist with the poorest of health, even with excruciating and persistent physical pain, if only these sufferings are viewed as God's Holy Will.

The point is, however, to what extent diseases can be related to the Will of God, and by what means a soul can reach such high moral perfection as to see God's Will in her physical ailments and lovingly embrace that Adorable Will.

No one is free to spend his health as he likes: to use or abuse it. On the contrary, everybody will render an account before God's tribunal of the use he has made of his health. The inference is plain: We have to take care of our body and its health, according to the rules of holy prudence. The masters of the spiritual life insist upon the so-called holy indifference in regard to our health, but their view should not be misinterpreted. As on the one hand, excessive interest in our body's welfare could degenerate into hypochondria, so again light-mindedness and imprudence in matters of health could easily impair or destroy that valuable gift of Divine Providence.

Most people know what to do and what to avoid, to preserve their health and ability for work. Experience will suggest to them many simple rules and means conducive to physical well-being and how to protect the body from unnecessary ailments. Eventually, whenever serious trouble develops in the body, medical care should not be disregarded. For, everybody is obliged to use reasonable measures to protect his health. Besides, those living under religious obedience are expected to keep their superiors informed about the general condition of their health. Should they notice some serious symptoms of disease, they must not conceal this from their superiors, not even with the intention of making a generous sacrifice of their health to God.

Despite all precautions, however, sickness overtakes many religious. Those enjoying permanent good health are but the few. It is, then, of special importance for their sanctification that they readily unite themselves with the Will of God in sickness. This Divine trial is, indeed, a touchstone of genuine abandonment to God, of moral perfection and sanctity. Whoever does not feel able to lovingly accept God's Will in time of sickness should not delude himself as to his spiritual progress. He is, at best, a beginner upon the way of perfection.

You may be tempted to regard sickness as a tragic handicap in the service of God, since you are not in a position to do useful work for your neighbors. You rather feel yourself a burden on the community. But why do you so easily forget that the thoughts of the Lord are not our thoughts? (*Is.* 55:8). Is it not infinitely more important to comply willingly with God's good pleasure than to be humanly useful to others? And what greater work can you achieve on earth than to show your neighbors an edifying example of wholehearted and loving surrender to the eternal decrees and designs of God?

However, you may rejoin: It is humanly impossible to give up health, to live a life of sadness and languor, while others enjoy the best of health and achieve marvels in the vineyard of the Lord...True, human nature left to itself cannot grasp the idea of leading an apparently useless life, accompanied moreover by incessant suffering. But the grace of God is certainly able to lift you above yourself, to permeate your heart with indomitable fortitude, that you may feel ready to sustain the most excruciating and protracted ailments with angelic and heroic patience, for the love of God.

Now, the point is that you must rely upon Divine grace and ask for it in continual and humble prayer. Unless you do this, no reasons and motives will prove sufficient to keep up your spirit and moral strength during a long and painful illness. Hence, if prayer is always a decisive factor in your spiritual life, even in good health and in the midst of success, then it is a hundredfold more important in the hour of cruel suffering. Unless you avail yourself of this omnipotent means, you have lost the spiritual combat. You will daily become more unhappy and you will lead a miserable existence.

To cooperate with the grace of the Holy Ghost in time of sickness, try to live up to the following rules:

First, never attempt to negotiate with God about the kind of ailment you are willing to endure, nor about the length of time it is to last. Instead, surrender yourself unconditionally to the Will of God and with childlike confidence entrust your future to His Wisdom and Goodness. Bargaining with God hints at a lack of confidence and of love for Him. God is pleased only with souls who wholeheartedly abandon themselves to Him.

Secondly, do not dispense yourself from prayer during your illness, under the pretext that prayer brings about fatigue and makes your condition worse. For one thing, this is untrue, generally speaking. Prayer, on the contrary, helps to preserve inner peace and thus it may greatly improve your health. Only long and exhausting devotions might harm your ailing body. Besides, even if prayer should result in temporary tiredness, it is so important and essential to your spiritual well-being in time of sickness, that you should faithfully fulfill this obligation regardless of the difficulties it may entail.

However, try to adapt your prayer to your physical condition. Let your prayer—during sickness—be very simple, like that of a child, let it be frequent and short rather than protracted and consequently exhausting. You certainly can be credited with perfect fidelity to prayer, if only during your illness you repeat acts of love and abandonment to God—let us say—several times an hour. These pious ejaculations may consist of some three or four simple words, or even can be offered without words. The only important thing is that your mind be lovingly turned to God, actually or virtually, in proportion to the amount of grace bestowed upon you by the Holy Ghost.

Thirdly, beware of giving bad example in any way to those within your environment; instead, make your illness a kind of an apostolate. If your visitors notice your loving surrender to the Divine Will, they are likely to profit spiritually each time they visit you. Your merit before God will increase daily. On the contrary, should your impatience or your excessive demands betray rather imperfect compliance with the Will of God, your influence upon visitors would certainly be negative.

One thing is sure: If you are wholeheartedly abandoned to God, the time of your sickness will be a golden period in your spiritual life.

14

PERMANENT INCAPACITY
FOR USEFUL WORK
MAY BE THE WILL OF GOD

Have you not looked, Dear Soul, with some kind of holy envy at certain servants of God, priests, religious or social workers, who endowed with remarkable gifts of nature and grace, achieved wonderful results in the field of their sacred ministry?

Has not sadness invaded your heart at times because of your incapacity for an effective apostolate, on account of your poor education, or because of other handicaps blocking your way to success? Perhaps, you even bore a shadow of grudge in your heart against Divine Providence, which so unequally distributes its favors and benefits.

Such sentiments are understandable, but certainly not warranted in a Christian, supernatural sense. For it is not the number and the value of talents received from God that decide our merits before God and the degree of our sanctity and of our glory in Heaven, but solely the perfection of our union with the Divine Will. A very simple soul may compete with the Seraphs in Heaven in love of God and sanctity, whereas others remain poor servants of God unto the very end, despite their wonderful capacities and opportunities.

The desire to accomplish great things for the glory of God and for the welfare of immortal souls is undoubtedly sublime and laudable. But to believe that such a goal can be reached only by persons endowed with extraordinary natural abilities and highly educated, is a mistake. Were all the Apostles, Martyrs, Confessors and other Saints of the Church, real geniuses, in the human sense of the term? No one has ever made such an assertion. And yet, the world's course of history has been radically changed by the Holy Apostles, and after them, the Saints of the Church have successfully continued their work, although most of them were not "great people" according to human standards.

The Maker of the universe, who calls into existence both simple daisies and magnificent roses—microscopic worms as well as the brave lion and the bold eagle—who creates the tiny grain of sand and the immense, almost immeasurable stars—is pleased in the wonderful varieties of souls. Each of them is destined to emphasize one Divine perfection, or rather one aspect of that perfection. Simplicity is predominant in some souls on account of their limited abilities. Others display charming beauty, both natural and supernatural, true masterpieces from God's hand. In a word, there are not two souls on earth perfectly alike as to spiritual, intellectual and physical qualities and endowments. This endless variety obviously depends upon God's eternal designs.

Now, insufficiently enlightened souls may feel despondent at the thought that, according to the immutable decrees of God, they must be and remain, in time and in eternity, but imperceptible grains of sand in the Kingdom of God. They surrender to the Divine Will, since there is no alternative for them. But they serve God in an atmosphere of gloomy thoughts and feelings, as if they were stepchildren of the Heavenly Father. . .

What a strange misunderstanding! No, there are no stepchildren in the Kingdom of God, either on earth or in Heaven. Every human soul, although poor and helpless, is called from eternity to a real and close union with God, that is to say, to an immensity of glory and happiness, beginning on earth and perfectly reaching her destination in eternity. And since the decisive and paramount means to attain that goal is God's grace which is never denied to souls of good will, the way to real greatness and to heavenly bliss is open to all.

The only condition to unite with God in His infinite glory and happiness is unwavering and loving compliance with His Sacred Will on earth, whatever one's position, capacities, endowments and activities may be. All the Saints of God unanimously insist upon the principle that it is better and more conducive to the glory of God and to the soul's happiness as well, to be a mere speck of dust in the universe by God's Will, than to resemble a very bright star apart from the Divine Will.

What comforting and sweet conclusions you can draw, Dear Soul, from this heavenly doctrine of Holy Church concerning the Holy Will of God and your union with it!

Perhaps you belong to that class of persons the world calls underprivileged, both in the natural and supernatural order. You feel yourself the poorest of the poor as far as intellectual capacities and education are concerned. The only thing you can do on earth is to fill a very common and ordinary place in human society, because your activity is restricted to simple physical work or other unimportant occupation. And yet, you are able to achieve great things for God's glory. If you are satisfied with your humble position, if you love it because it is God's Will, if your only striving is to comply perfectly with the good pleasure of God, then you certainly can count yourself among the closest friends of

the Divine Heart. And so you are greater in
God's eyes than geniuses who have astonished
the world by their achievements, but have ignored the good pleasure of God.

Inability for humanly useful work sets in at
times unexpectedly. Perhaps you have been working very successfully for years in the field of
education, of charity, of social organizations, or
directly for the salvation and sanctification of
souls; then, a serious sickness disables you permanently, both for intellectual and for physical
work. At best, you can give only limited service
to others, especially when your inability is due
to your advancing age. If this is your case, beware of mistaking the situation and the good
pleasure of God. You may be tempted to despondency, yet you have not the least reason to give
way to gloomy thoughts and sentiments.

As a rule, it is the Will of God that souls called
to perfection cease working externally, or at least
drastically restrict their activities, toward the end
of their earthly career, thus being able to supplement the deficiency of their spiritual life. To
make His good pleasure more certain and clear,
God often deprives them completely of all the
necessary capacities and physical health. According to human standards, they start a period of
useless existence. No wonder, then, that despondency and sadness set in, at least temporarily,
until the sufferer is able to understand the de-

signs of Divine Providence and eventually is reconciled with his new condition, humiliating and painful for nature, but very salutary for his sanctification.

How thankful you should be to God, Dear Soul, that you are called upon to occupy your mind and heart almost exclusively with things Divine and eternal! This will enable you to love God more, to unite with Him more closely and thus to advance in sanctity more rapidly than was possible when you were on active duty. Without this period of apparent inactivity, your spiritual progress would probably remain short of the goal God has ordained for you from eternity.

Never yield to the temptation that now you are a useless member of the Church, of your religious Community. In fact, during this contemplative, passive period of your life you have a much more important and more sublime task before you than formerly. Like Saint Therese of the Child Jesus, you are to pray, to suffer and to love God for those who believe themselves to be too busy to devote sufficient time to the direct service of God. In this manner you may become incomparably more useful to souls now than you were at any time in the past.

The point to observe is: you must readily embrace God's Will, as it is manifested to you from day to day, from moment to moment, with boundless, seraphic love.

15

WRONGS AND INJURIES YOU SUFFER ARE THE WILL OF GOD

No sin, no injustice, no moral imperfection whatsoever may be directly related to God, who is eternal and infinite Sanctity. Hence, whenever people are consciously unjust to you, so as to offend God thereby, they cannot consider their acts the Will of God. They are deliberately opposing the Will of God. However, this is only one side of the picture.

When you consider, so to say, the reverse of the medal, any kind of injustice will appear to your eyes as an event conformable to the Will of God. This is true when you consider *your* side of the injustice. In other words, as the sinner who persecutes a just soul undoubtedly offends God, so the victim of persecution is certainly complying with the Will of God while he patiently and peacefully endures the wrong.

Most people, even those striving for perfection, contemplate the injustice inflicted upon them, so to say, from the wrong side. Instead of asking what God wants them to do, to think and to feel at the time of the injustice, they rather angrily and persistently inquire why people commit that injustice. Now it is God who has reserved for Himself the right to judge and to sentence the persecutor; the victim's only obligation is peacefully to suffer the inflicted evils. That is to say that any wrong done to a person must be accepted by the innocent sufferer as the manifest Will of God.

Human nature, created to the likeness of God, and basically good, keenly resents every kind of injustice. However, enlightened souls are always mindful of the truth that man, after Original Sin, has only a very restricted right to complain about the hardships of life. Should he even be subjected to every possible wrong and injustice on earth, still his debt to God would be greater than all his sufferings combined. Does not revelation teach us that one mortal sin deserves eternal punishment in Hell? Consequently, refrain from viewing your little earthly afflictions and adversities as wrongs done to you. You often repeat this humble prayer: My fault, my fault, my most grievous fault...Be consistent, then, and do not take the alleged wrongs you suffer too tragically.

Striving for religious sanctity is tantamount to following in the footsteps of Our Lord Jesus Christ. If you have left this goal out of your sight, then you have definitely wandered from the path of evangelical perfection, if not from the way of salvation. Now, who on earth has ever suffered wrongs comparable to those inflicted upon the Innocent Lamb of God, the Only-Begotten Son of the Eternal Father, absolutely equal to Him in sanctity? Jesus was not only ignored and despised by the leaders of Israel, but accused of revolt against the Law of God, of falsehood, of pride, of blasphemy. As a result, He was publicly executed on the gallows of the Cross, between two notorious thieves. All this took place after countless and manifest miracles wrought by the Saviour in testimony of His Divine mission and of the truth of His doctrine.

How is it possible that souls, contemplating the Passion and the Death of Jesus Christ, and striving for perfection, can protest so bitterly against the alleged wrongs inflicted upon them? Are they not renouncing real religious sanctity by doing so?

We agree that patient and peaceful surrender to unjust treatment inflicted by our neighbor does not necessarily mean complete indifference and absolute passivity. Even Jesus, our Divine Model, protested at times against injuries and wrongs, though always in a very mild and peaceful manner. Whether to suffer in silence, or to take necessary measures for self-defense, depends upon circumstances. But one thing is sure: The more fervent a soul is in the service of God, and the higher the sanctity she is tending toward—the more reasons she finds to imitate Jesus by remaining silent before the tribunals of unjust authorities. A soul sincerely abandoned to God will prudently and peacefully defend her cause only in instances when her conscience urges her to do so. And this happens rather seldom.

And do you know, Dear Soul, what constitutes the most effective self-defense? It consists above all in humble silence, unlimited patience and special kindness toward those who are responsible for your sufferings. Individuals vociferous in their self-defense are seldom right and rarely innocent. On the contrary, the religious who confides his cause to Divine Providence and consequently refrains from all violent measures and words of self-defense, is sooner or later found to be right. Try this excellent method. It is not the easiest of all, but with God's grace you are able to practice even heroic virtue.

What is the source of that super-human force that enables saintly souls to bear patiently, or even joyfully, every kind of wrong, mistreatment and adversity? It is their childlike, ardent love of God. Love is as strong as death, according to the word of the Holy Ghost. (*Cant.* 8:6). If this is true—to a certain extent—even in genuine human love, then it is a thousand times more applicable to ardent love of God. No wonder, then, that really pious and fervent souls, who thoroughly grasp the transcendent value and importance, the depth and sublimity of the love of God, are never worried or troubled in the presence of adversities and of injuries inflicted upon them. At times, they even sincerely enjoy the precious privilege of being treated unjustly, like Jesus, their only love.

Should you realize from what has been said that your spiritual condition is quite different from that of the perfect children of God, from the thoughts and feelings of Jesus Himself, then thoroughly examine your conscience to find out what your principal infidelities and spiritual shortcomings are. In all probability, you have a poor spirit of prayer, and as a result, your love toward God is far from being tender, ardent and perfect. And that is certainly the reason why you are not too enthusiastic about imitating Jesus, carrying His Cross and dying upon Calvary. To remedy the situation, waste no time. Resolve today to recommence a true life of prayer, of continual recollection in God's presence, so as to obtain the inestimable grace of perfect love toward God. Once you achieve this goal, your courage in bearing wrongs will grow amazingly. You will be able to love your real or imaginary enemies sincerely.

This problem of learning how to bear peacefully and calmly all manner of mistreatment and real injustice is absolutely essential to your sanctification. Ideal justice will never materialize on earth, not even in very fervent convents, among perfect and saintly souls. As long as the human mind is fallible and natural self-love confuses the clarity of its judgments, so long will disputes be inevitable among men and injustice, deliberate or otherwise, must occur in some form or other. Hence, absolute equity insisted upon in Community life would only engender continuous strife, recriminations and all kinds of trouble. The only way to lasting peace, both in our soul and in our Community, is described by Our Lord Himself in these words: "Learn of me, because I am meek and humble of heart." (*Matt.* 11:29).

Indeed, blessed are those who begin to resemble Jesus, the meekest Lamb of God.

16

THE WILL OF GOD IN HUMILIATIONS

What touches the most sensitive spot in human nature is humiliation, no matter under what form it may appear. Usually the more a soul deserves humiliation, the less she proves willing to accept trials. Whereas saintly souls, encouraged by the Divine example of their despised and crucified Saviour, are able to preserve peace of heart in the midst of the most unjust humiliations. Imperfect people and sinners are out of balance each time they believe themselves to be treated with too little consideration and respect.

To comply with the Will of God in humiliations requires truly superhuman virtue, particularly when humiliations are or seem to be undeserved and unjust. In fact, it takes a very advanced religious to face all kinds of humiliation with imperturbable peace. But those who have attained this degree of perfection are probably mounting the very summit of heroic sanctity. Religious who do not feel called to heroic virtue are expected—at least—to control their sensitiveness at the moment of humiliation, so

as to avoid scandalous outbursts of resentment
and anger. If they feel upset temporarily, they
should try to regain their inner balance by means
of humble prayer. If they fail to pray, they
themselves are at fault when pride has been the
conqueror.

Certain unfaithful religious may maintain that
humiliations are not reconcilable with human
dignity, with respect due to their actual position. Moreover, they will angrily protest against
any kind of public humiliation. When such opinions and feelings take root and spread in a Community, then true spiritual life, perfection and
sanctity cannot survive for any length of time.
For, there is no real humility without humiliations, and humility is one of the fundamental
virtues of the religious life and of Christian perfection. Consequently, all false conceptions of
human dignity and honor must be eliminated
from the mind of a religious, at any cost.

No doubt, the dignity of every human being,
as a child of God, is very great, in a certain sense
immeasurable, as far as its eternal destination is
concerned. But humiliations do not affect man's
real dignity. The latter is impaired only by deeds,
words or even thoughts and feelings of the individual himself if they are unbecoming for a
child of God. Whatever other people think and
say about us or do against us, leaves our dignity
intact when the objections launched against our

personality are groundless.

A good reputation is a very precious boon, particularly to those called to social, educational or apostolic work. Whenever one's good name is questionable, people must lose confidence in all his actions and teachings. Hence, religious are not only entitled to watch over their good reputation, but are obliged to do so. They are particularly expected to shun anything that might impair or ruin that reputation. This obvious obligation concerning one's reputation is sometimes advanced as a pretext for not accepting humiliations which are inflicted upon religious, by equals or even by superiors. However, not even the person directly involved sincerely believes that humiliation actually destroys his good name. It is rather his reaction to humiliations that may affect his reputation.

There is no better example to encourage us to willingly accept humiliations than that of Jesus hanging upon the Cross. What does that Cross signify? It is the gallows of ancient times. . . And who is executed upon it? Jesus, true God and true man. . . God omnipotent and of infinite Majesty dying upon the gallows!. . . Can you conceive a word or phrase in human language which would even approximately express the humiliation involved in this appalling crime and tragedy? . . . And Jesus submits in silence. Instead of protesting against the most terrible humiliation ever inflicted upon an innocent person, Jesus utters this astonishing prayer before His last breath: "Father, forgive them, for they know not what they do." (*Luke* 23:34).

For Our Beloved Lord, His whole Passion and death was the manifest Will of His heavenly Father. He clearly expressed this during His agony in the Garden of Olives: "Father. . . not my will, but thine be done." (*Luke* 22:42). No commentator of Holy Writ, no saintly writer, no enlightened Christian ever questioned the fact that Jesus regarded His Passion and death, His inconceivable humiliation on Calvary, as the Will of His Father. And that is why He so lovingly submitted to His fate.

No religious soul should delude herself that she is following in the footsteps of Jesus upon the way of perfection and sanctity, unless she is animated, at least to a certain extent, with the spirit of genuine humility as shown in the Person of Our Crucified Redeemer. And she certainly is lacking in that spirit, if she refuses to accept humiliations, silently, whether actually deserved or not. To submit only to righteous humiliations amounts, indeed, only to a certain degree of justice. Perfect humility is practiced only when just and unjust humiliations are silently accepted.

You may object and say: Yes, but Jesus was the Victim of expiation for all mankind, according to the eternal designs of His heavenly Father. I am a simple servant of God. Hence, I do not feel obliged to participate in His humiliations, since I am not responsible for the sins of other people, and do not feel too guilty myself before God...

Now, is that the language of fervent and saintly souls? Are you, indeed, free from every responsibility regarding the sins of mankind? Does not the Holy Ghost Himself encourage you to "fill up those things that are wanting of the sufferings of Christ" (*Col.* 1:24), as did St. Paul, the Apostle? Your love toward God would in fact appear very doubtful, should you dispense yourself from all participation in the atonement for the iniquities of the world. And as to your alleged innocence before God, be rather cautious in assuming it. For, according to the revealed doctrine, one deliberate venial sin is sufficient reason to humiliate yourself and to do penance all your life. And even then you would not be able adequately to atone for this single offense against God. And what is your position before God's sanctity and justice, if you are guilty of one or more mortal sins? It is eternal punishment in Hell that you have deserved.

"But it is so hard, nay, almost humanly impossible to accept repeated humiliations again and again, as they are inflicted in the common religious life and under holy obedience! I cannot take this gloomy kind of life. . ." some cowardly people may rejoin.

In fact, genuine humility has traits of heroism. It is a very difficult, superhuman virtue. But nothing proves impossible to those who rely upon the grace of God and incessantly ask for it in humble prayer. Besides, a humble life is by no means a gloomy, unbearable life. The first humiliations you encounter and try to accept as God's Holy Will may cost you much. But each time you conquer your proud nature, peace and heavenly joy will flood your heart. Then, as you are more deeply rooted in humility, you will wonder why it was so difficult for you formerly to comply with the Divine Will in humiliations. With abundant grace of the Holy Ghost you may reach that degree of perfection when you will rejoice with the Saints that you "were accounted worthy to suffer reproach for the name of Jesus." (*Acts* 5:41).

What a desirable goal! You may readily achieve it if only you try consistently and valiantly to accept every kind of humiliation as the Holy Will of God.

17

THE DEGREE OF YOUR SANCTITY IS DETERMINED BY GOD'S HOLY WILL

"This is the will of God, your sanctification," (*1 Thess.* 4:3), says the Holy Spirit. And no Christian has ever doubted that the main purpose of our earthly life consists in perfecting our resemblance to God by continual progress in virtue. But as to the degree and extent of sanctification, revelation is too often misunderstood, even by some religious. It is almost commonly believed that God has left it to the decision of each soul to determine the degree of sanctity she wants to attain and the sort of sanctity that best appeals to her heart. Now, this is certainly a false conception.

There are no mere accidents in the whole universe. Whatever comes to pass in the physical sphere is due to one of the laws that govern earth and Heaven, according to the eternal Will of the Creator. How can it be assumed, then, that in the supernatural realm of grace things are only generally outlined, all details being left to man's will and preference? As if God was more interested in the perfection of the material order than in affairs supernatural and eternal.

It is true, man is endowed by God with free will, and this fact must be taken into account in discussing the problems of Divine grace, of man's sanctification and salvation. This means that in the relationship of man to God, things cannot happen with physical necessity as in the material world. However, it would be a great mistake to assume that God, Infinite Wisdom, had no definite and elaborate plan as to the spiritual life of souls, but that He has left it to their will to choose the degree and the kind of sanctity and of heavenly glory they are to attain. God is the absolute Master of all creatures, of their fate in time and in eternity, and He will not renounce and cannot renounce even the minutest part of His omnipotence and His eternal prerogatives, if this word may be used in reference to God.

No doubt, God by a decree of His adorable Will has from all eternity fixed the degree of sanctity and of glory each human soul is to attain by the right use of her free will, with the assistance of the necessary grace. Though it should not be forgotten even for a moment that God's absolute, omnipotent domination in the order of grace does not abolish or destroy man's free will. The relationship and cooperation between God's omnipotent grace and our free will

can neither be adequately conceived nor explained
by the mind of man. For God is incomprehensible both in His essence and in His creative
activity.

Outstanding masters of spirituality repeatedly
warn all souls called to perfection, particularly
religious, against the evil consequences of opposition to the Will of God, as also to the manifest wishes of the Divine Heart. While certain
kinds of such opposition are by no means sinful, they always are bound to impair the soul's
relationship to God. At least, this relationship
will become cooler and cooler, and as a result,
the service of God must grow more difficult for
the unfaithful soul. Who can tell whether she
will persevere until the end in meeting her strict
obligations? Even a complete estrangement from
God is possible as a consequence of deliberate
and protracted opposition to the inspirations of
the Holy Ghost.

Bear constantly in mind, Dear Soul, these
words of the Apostle: "This is the will of God,
your sanctification" (*1 Thess.* 4:3) and beware of
putting an arbitrary meaning to this declaration
of the Holy Spirit. Your sanctification must reach
the goal previsioned by Divine Providence; you
cannot consult your ease and comfort and stop
on a lower level of perfection. For, the last and
decisive word in regard to your sanctification
and your future glory in Heaven is obviously

· with God, not with you. And yet remember that only loving and cheerful compliance with the Will of God is able to complete your sanctification and your blissful union with the Supreme Good. Therefore take the road of true fervor in God's service unhesitatingly and wholeheartedly, and if you feel yourself lovingly and insistently urged to greater sanctity, do not refuse the invitation. The alternative—to say the least—would mean a rather gloomy outlook for your happiness in the service of God.

Those not adequately enlightened in spiritual matters at times feel discouraged on the way of perfection, chiefly because they have not made sure that God actually wants them to advance in sanctity, to become saints. Never yield, Dear Soul, to this treacherous temptation. If you take time to study the treatises of outstanding, saintly theologians on the various degrees of perfection and sanctity, you will realize that they all agree upon this principle: Every Christian soul is called by God to that degree of sanctity which she is able to grasp and can actually attain, having at her disposal all necessary supernatural graces and lights. . . And they give this reason: God never does anything without a purpose. So, if He bestows abundant light upon a soul concerning her sanctity, and grants her sufficient courage to strive for it, there can be no doubt as to this soul's call to the very heights of sanctity.

At any cost, then, make sure that you are in perfect accord with God's eternal Will as to your sanctification.

In one sense, you are free to decide the degree of sanctity you are to aspire to, but in another sense, you are not free in this regard. As far as Canon Law, ecclesiastical and religious regulations are concerned, you meet all your obligations by avoiding direct transgressions of your vows, of your rule and of all other religious duties and customs. But while complying with their strict obligations in the religious life, religious may differ greatly from one another as to the degree of inner, or even outer perfection when they work and pray, or perform various acts of virtue. Now, while people are wholly satisfied with your orderly life, God may find less complacency in you and your perfection, because He expects greater sanctity from you, perhaps even heroic sanctity. True enough, you are in accord with the Divine Will inasmuch as you consistently shun grievous and venial sin in the service of God. You are a good religious.

If it has never occurred to your mind that you could strive after higher perfection—if you see no reason for exerting yourself more than necessary—if you are not able to grasp the meaning of higher sanctity—if you have never felt any uneasiness in your conscience on account of your restricted spiritual aspirations—then you

may not be called to closer friendship with God.
You may not receive the necessary light and
graces. But if your inner experience is just the
opposite of what has been described above, that
is to say, if both the external circumstances of
your past life and the frequent inspirations of
the Holy Ghost urge you to set a much higher
goal for yourself in the spiritual life, and moreover, if your spiritual guides also insist upon your
striving for higher sanctity—then there is hardly
a doubt that God is not yet entirely satisfied
with your spiritual state. In all probability, your
will is not in perfect accord with the wishes of
the Divine Heart, with the eternal designs of
God, concerning your sanctification and your
heavenly glory.

A soul who consciously fails to exert herself
beyond her strict obligations is certainly not
guilty of sin. To some extent, she may be termed
"perfect," and yet there may be a shade of guilt
on her conscience inasmuch as she is not sufficiently faithful and docile to the grace of God.
In fact, is it not a striking imperfection, an infidelity to God, to refuse obedience when God
calls a soul to higher sanctity? Is God not free
to determine the degree of sanctity and glory
He wants us to attain?

18

HOLY OBEDIENCE, THE CLEAREST MANIFESTATION OF THE DIVINE WILL

By "obedience" we mean its object, its extent, all the obligations it imposes upon those bound in religion by the vow of obedience. Let it be stressed, however, that even non-religious superiors and legitimate authorities are representatives of God, for their respective subjects, and consequently are to be obeyed as heralds of the Divine Will, within certain conditions and restrictions. Did not Jesus, the Son of God, defer to legitimate Jewish and heathen authorities?

There is hardly another rule in the entire spiritual life so unanimously agreed upon by theologians and ascetical writers as the statement that prompt and willing obedience to all commands and legitimate wishes of the superiors is the main touchstone of religious perfection and genuine sanctity. And the reason is obvious and clear. The orders of legitimate superiors unmistakably manifest the Will of God. And sanctity means nothing but childlike, wholehearted love of the Divine Will, both in theory and in practice.

Whatever the moral qualities of a religious, if he is not in accord with holy obedience, his apparent perfection has very limited value with God, if any at all. For, he is doing his own will instead of God's Will, and is more interested in his personal comfort than in the good pleasure of God. In other words, obedience, its promptitude and general perfection, is a very reliable measure of the spiritual progress of religious souls.

Religious obedience, however, as the manifestation of God's Will, is conditioned not only by the legal position of the respective superiors, but by the character of their particular demands as well. The authority of religious superiors is by no means unlimited. It extends only as far as is specified either by Canon Law or by the special constitutions of the community. Religious obedience must be connected with the proper religious life, that is to say, with the holy vows, with the religious rule and with established religious customs. Anything that has no bearing upon the religious life and religious perfection— say, adherence to some rather innocuous political, social, or scientific opinion—cannot be imposed upon the subjects in the name of holy obedience. It is to be emphasized, however, that in the case of a doubt whether certain directions of the superiors are related to the religious life or not, all subjects are bound in conscience to acquiesce in the decision of their superiors. Otherwise the many subterfuges on the part of lukewarm religious would almost make a mockery of obedience in communities.

It stands to reason that no precept of a superior can be binding if the command is undoubtedly and evidently sinful, as no sin, grievous or venial, can ever be the Will of God. "Undoubtedly and evidently sinful". . . Here again the principle applies stated above that in a case of doubt the superior, not the subject, is entitled to decide. While the doubt remains, obedience binds in conscience.

Excepting these cases when a superior evidently exceeds the limits of his power, or when his command is evidently sinful, the subject must obey. However, in such matters as are expressly exempt from the jurisdiction of religious superiors by Canon Law, like "matter of conscience"—the power of the superior ceases. Obedience binds, without doubt, even in cases when the directions of the superiors are imprudent, impracticable, imperfect. While every subject is entitled humbly and deferentially to explain to his superiors about the inconvenience or danger connected with the precept issued, he may never refuse obedience, if the superiors insist upon their decision. Should he refuse, he is manifestly opposing the Will of God.

Alas, human nature is extremely ingenious in

discovering reasons for evading obedience in practice. Theoretically, of course, every religious highly appreciates obedience and would never question the principles that obedience constitutes the very core of religious sanctity. Even those obviously lukewarm in the service of God and often reluctant in carrying out the directions of their superiors pretend as a rule that they faithfully keep the vow of obedience. As to the frequent troubles in their relation with religious authorities, they will blame anything and anybody in the world except themselves. According to their opinion, almost everything is wrong in the field of obedience and religious administration. Superiors are said to be incompetent. Supposedly, they demand excessive, servile submission, without taking account of the critical remarks made by experienced subjects. Imperfections in obedience, say the malcontents, are exaggerated by the superiors who cling to their positions and power. Many other presumptuous remarks of the same kind are made to excuse the reluctant and proud attitude of unfaithful religious toward the representatives of God and toward the Will of God.

Souls sincerely abandoned to God always respect authority. They never indulge even in critical thoughts against their superiors. Though their opinion might differ from that of the superiors, they control their natural pride and are always mindful of human fallibility. They know and feel that they have no authority to pass judgment on the deeds of their superiors. Souls faithful to God and to the vow of obedience will carefully beware of bitter sentiments against the representatives of God and their directions. While they cannot always prevent such feelings, they will not deliberately assent to them, nor will they consciously nourish or stir them up. And above all, in keeping with their holy profession, fervent religious never outwardly oppose their superiors, as this may easily result in public scandal and thus do considerable harm to the respective community and often leads to formal sin. Souls who deeply grasp the sense of their vow of obedience are thoroughly permeated with the truth that the will of their superiors is the Will of God, whatever the shortcomings of the superiors or of their administrative methods.

It is absolutely essential to supernatural obedience to see God's Will in all the commands of legitimate authority. Submission from natural, doubtful or evidently low motives is valueless in the eyes of God. It is even unbecoming to man's personal dignity. Only real Christian obedience that submits rather to God in the person of His representatives than to man as man is a sublime virtue, able rather to enhance human dignity than to impair it.

The perfection of religious obedience and its

merit for eternity increases proportionately as the particular acts of obedience are related more directly and more lovingly to God, and to His Holy Will. The simplest actions in God's service become sublime acts of Divine love and consequently effectively further the soul's sanctification, if the soul is exclusively interested in complying with the Will of God as manifested in holy obedience. The conclusion is obvious, namely, that perfect supernatural obedience scarcely differs from actual sanctity.

So St. Alphonsus Liguori is undoubtedly right when in one of his little poems he repeats this seraphic refrain: O how worthy of love thou art, O Holy Will of God! . . .

19

ON THE WORDS OF THE APOSTLE: "WE OUGHT TO OBEY GOD RATHER THAN MEN" (*Acts* 5:29)

Yes, God is to be obeyed more, infinitely more, than men. Christian obedience is essentially related to God, the eternal Source of all authority. Consequently, obedience can never be binding in conscience if it is evidently not in accord with the Will of God.

No Christian maxim is more certain, simple and clear than this. And yet, it is too often misinterpreted by persons who wish to evade obedience at any cost. To obey God directly is obviously easier, or seems to be easier, than to submit to the commands of the representatives of God. Generally, the Will of God, considered apart from ordinary religious obedience, is subject to arbitrary interpretation and is often made to fit the likes and dislikes of everyone. Thus, the supposed Will of God is a tempting pretext for independent action, notwithstanding the vow of obedience.

When you pretend to comply with God's Will,

and oppose religious obedience, you refer, not to a special revelation, but to your own conscience. "My conscience is the voice of God"— you say—"therefore I am obliged to follow its dictates." Indeed, you are right in your general assertion that you must obey your conscience as a harbinger of the Divine Will. However, have you made sure that you are not mistaking your wishful thinking for the dictates of your conscience and Will of God? The dictates of conscience are not synonymous with your private personal opinion. Real certitude as to the Will of God is necessary. In other words, you may and must follow your conscience, whatever the dictates of religious obedience, if you cannot doubt the Will of God in certain circumstances. Then, and only then your duty is evident "to obey God rather than men."

Actually, the case will seldom be so simple and clear as to warrant and to justify your opposition to obedience because of the dictates of your conscience, as a manifestation of the Divine Will. As a rule, your conscience only *seems* to forbid your complying with the demands of obedience. As a matter of fact, you are rather uneasy and hesitant, as the arguments in favor of your conscience and liberty are doubtful. In such circumstances no religious bound by the vow of obedience may refuse submission.

Lukewarm, relaxed religious frequently make

themselves believe that they have sufficient or even urgent reasons to contradict or to disregard the orders of their superiors, because, they say, "God must be obeyed rather than men." On the contrary, saintly servants of God find this to be true only in very exceptional cases, when they encounter some difficulties in the field of obedience. Now, who is right, the docile or the recalcitrant religious? We feel that all those acquainted with the religious life know the right answer.

If you sincerely wish, Dear Soul, safely to go along the road leading to Heaven and to real sanctity, beware above all of your treacherous self that hates every kind of submission, even adherence to the Will of God as revealed by holy obedience. Consistently try to control and to conquer your natural pride, which is the arch-enemy of obedience and sanctity. Do not pay attention to the bad example you may notice around you. On the contrary, the more your imperfect and unfaithful companions transgress against humble obedience, the more willingness try to show in obeying your superiors, thus to atone to Our Lord for others. You will feel yourself growing in happiness.

Probably, temptations against obedience will assail you from time to time, particularly during periods of aridity, spiritual darkness and despondency. You will be reminded of your age, your experience, your merits, your qualities. Why should you—the temptation will insist—be always treated as a helpless child? Are you not able to form an opinion and pass a judgment without the assistance of your superiors? You have your own conscience which you are entitled to follow, since your superiors are far from being infallible or perfect. Is it not naive and stupid to comply silently with all the wishes of those vested with power which easily can be misused and, in fact, often is misused?...To withstand all such temptations, abundant grace of God is indispensable. Therefore, ask humbly and perseveringly for that grace in prayer.

Should you find yourself, exceptionally, in a situation where opposition on your part against the wishes of your superiors would seem inevitable, be very careful before making a positive decision. However, if in the past your obedience was always blameless, if you feel yourself sincerely interested only in the Will of God, and finally, if your regular director of conscience assures you that you are correct in your opinion, then you may unquestionably follow the dictates of your conscience rather than the wishes of your superiors. If this happens only occasionally there is no reason for worry. You are correctly applying the principle: "We ought to obey God rather than men."

To be elaborate on this subject, let us illustrate by an example:

You are entrusted with an important task in your community by your superiors. You feel you should earnestly exert yourself in your work, whether administrative, educational, charitable or otherwise, to comply with the wishes of your superiors. And, thank God, deeply rooted in the virtue of obedience, you do your best. Now, suppose the amount of work increases daily, until you are physically and even morally approaching the breaking point. Your conscience is alarmed because you realize that your spiritual life is evidently weakening. After weeks of excessive work you feel not only utterly exhausted, but so nervous that you can hardly pray. Despondency threatens to overcome your soul. No wonder, your conscience is alarmed.

Finally, since the superiors disregard your complaints you decide after long and ardent prayer, and after consulting your spiritual guide, that you must restrict your work to what is humanly possible, without neglecting your spiritual life, or endangering your sanctification. Accordingly, you adopt a new method in your work. You try to meet all the wishes of your superiors, but if this is not possible, and you leave a part of your work undone, you remain quiet in conscience. You are mindful of the rule that "God must be obeyed rather than men." And you feel certain that you would disobey your conscience and God Himself, if you should continue to do the work of two or three persons, and thus endanger your spiritual life only to please your superiors.

Are you right in the case? Yes, you are. Perfectly right. The Will of God here is unquestionable. Your superiors have overestimated your physical and moral capacities. They should be obeyed nevertheless, but only as far as actually possible.

Let us add, however, that even in instances where your opposition to obedience is inevitable, the form of the opposition must be in accord with religious humility and with respect due to the representatives of God. An insolent attitude toward superiors, striking and numerous as their defects may be, is never reconcilable with genuine religious perfection and sanctity. It signifies pride, and pride is bound to infect and radically destroy all spiritual, supernatural life.

20

ON THE WORDS OF OUR LORD: "HE THAT HEARETH YOU, HEARETH ME; AND HE THAT DESPISETH YOU, DESPISETH ME" (*Luke* 10:16)

Again and again this text is referred to whenever religious souls are encouraged to perfect and willing obedience. Indeed, no more effective motive for obedience can be advanced than this solemn declaration of the Son of God. True, it was addressed directly to the Apostles when they were sent to preach the Holy Gospel to all creatures. But there is not the least doubt as to its general application in relationship between subjects and superiors, as must be gathered from the consensus of all Catholic theologians and writers. The Saints of God are more than positive in applying these words to holy obedience in general.

But even if this declaration had not been made, formally and expressly, by Our Divine Master, there would be no doubt that our obedience or disobedience goes back to God Himself, who has vested all superiors with authority. People who oppose the lower officials of the adminis-

116

tration are really opposing the supreme ruler of the nation. This principle applies all the more to religious superiors, who must be regarded as representatives of Christ. Opposition to them is opposition to Christ, the Head of His Church and of all religious communities as parts of the Church. In other words, those who obey their superiors, obey Christ Himself; those opposed to obedience are in opposition to Christ, the Divine Source of religious authority.

Self-confident and self-willed individuals may remark that the Apostles were worthy and saintly representatives of Christ and because of their sanctity, the Divine Master told them: He that heareth you, heareth Me...Ordinary superiors, they object, are often devoid of the qualities indispensable to representatives of God. Therefore, they maintain, the declaration of Christ does not apply to them.

If this interpretation should be correct, how could Our Lord tell His audience, referring to the Pharisees: "Whatsoever they shall say to you, observe and do: but according to their works, do ye not: for they say, and do not." (*Matt.* 23:3). The Pharisees, contemporaries of Christ, were the worst type of superiors. Nevertheless, Jesus insists upon obedience due to them as representatives of His Heavenly Father. It follows, beyond any doubt, that subjects are not entitled to pass judgment about the worthiness or unworthiness of their superiors, but are bound to comply with their directions and precepts as if coming from God Himself. He who obeys the superiors, obeys God. He who despises them, in a certain sense, despises God Himself.

The words of Our Lord: "He that heareth you, heareth Me" always were and are a sweet comfort to souls who are animated only with one great, insatiable desire to love God with their whole heart and with seraphic ardor; they desire to comply as perfectly as possible with God's good pleasure, and long to be united with Him even here on earth, but at times are subject to anxieties of conscience, on account of doubts which often arise as to the real Will of God. These afflicted souls may be sure that God is watching them with special complacency and is drawing them closer and closer to His own Heart. They need only to obey with childlike simplicity and love, carrying out the wishes and desires of their superiors. For, then, they are lovingly embracing the Holy Will of God.

Our whole spiritual life would inevitably be a troubled and uneasy one if we did not know, by Our Lord's express declaration, that those who obey their superiors are obeying God Himself and undoubtedly are doing His Will. A great many souls enter religious communities chiefly for one special reason. In the convent, under holy obedience, they will always know, exactly and certainly, what God wants them to do, whatever the circumstances. This happy condition of soul will be for them a source of supernatural peace and of heavenly bliss. Yes, the religious life, under strict obedience, is a real and great sacrifice. But it brings its own reward in the form of sweet supernatural peace.

How regrettable it is that some religious souls deliberately deprive themselves of that precious reward and of a considerable part of their merits, because only too often they forget the Divine declaration: "He that heareth you, heareth Me"!...If they are not encouraged to obedience by these words, they should at least recall the warning that follows: "He that despiseth you, despiseth Me." Presumably, no religious, not even the most lukewarm, would dare despise Jesus, the Only-Begotten Son of God. Yet, they are told expressly by Him that they are doing so— semi-consciously, let us hope—whenever they refuse deference and obedience to their superiors on account of their alleged defects and general unworthiness.

It is only too easy for human weakness to discover all kinds of imperfections and faults in the personality and manner of superiors whom one dislikes and whose directions do not appeal to our natural pride and self-will. For, then conscience is easily appeased and silenced, despite striking infidelities in matters of holy obedience.

In these circumstances, you may be tempted to believe that you are not expected to obey such superiors strictly. But if you let yourself be deceived by this fallacy, do you not feel in the depth of your heart that you are despising the representatives of Christ? Can you expect God's assistance and blessing in your spiritual life? Can you feel happy in your holy vocation?

No superior on earth is absolutely faultless and perfect. Some may even show a great lack of virtue or prudence. Hence, no religious need regard his superiors as true saints and as ideals of perfection because vested with authority, especially when there are too many indications to the contrary. It proves impossible, even to souls animated with the deepest spirit of humility, charity and obedience, to see nothing but virtue, perfection and wisdom in the life and in the administrative methods of some superiors. And they are not obliged to do violence to their own reason and to evident facts, and to persuade themselves that their superiors are perfect. For, even should they try, they could not sincerely believe it.

However, realizing the shortcomings and mistakes of superiors is not tantamount to despising God's representatives or slighting their authority. It means nothing more than yielding to evident facts. It implies theoretical disapproval of deeds or orders which no one can recognize as right and perfect. Only when such criticism results in voluntary bitterness toward the superiors, or in external irreverence, or in a reluctance to obey, then the malcontent can no longer reconcile his attitude with the spirit of religious obedience. Then the warning of Our Lord can be aptly applied: "He that despiseth you, despiseth Me."

It is to be stressed, however, that enlightened and saintly religious manage, as a rule, to excuse the apparent faults or mistakes of their superiors. True humility and charity urge fervent subjects to attribute short-sightedness, ignorance, or bias to themselves. At least, they never indulge in public criticism of their superiors, since this would undoubtedly constitute a fault against the reverence due to all representatives of God, and would inevitably cause scandal to others. And actual scandal is sinful.

21

HOW SAINTLY SUPERIORS VIEW THE WILL OF GOD IN OBEDIENCE

Those vested with authority in religious communities find themselves in a rather delicate situation as far as holy obedience is concerned. On the one hand, they are entitled and even obliged to preserve and to protect their authority over the respective religious family; and on the other hand, they are expected to become models of humility, of forebearance and charity to their subjects. Since obedience is a hard virtue for everybody, superiors are supposed to take all possible measures to facilitate it in daily life. Let us see how they can achieve this goal without demeaning their character as representatives of God.

The Catholic doctrine concerning religious obedience states that superiors are to dwell upon the basic truth that the religious regime is by no means democratic, in the common sense of the term. It is rather theocratic, in a broad sense, inasmuch as all religious authority is to be referred to Christ and to God—much more directly than the authority vested in civil powers.

As democracy means government by the people and for the people, so religious government is enacted in the name of God and for the glory of God. Indeed, a regime approaching real theocracy, as seen in the history of Israel, at the time of the Prophets. Democracy in religious communities is found only in the form of humility, simplicity, condescension.

Perfect superiors certainly insist, as they must, upon submission to their directions, not because it is their own will or wish, but because it is undoubtedly the Will of God that all subjects comply with their orders. The form of this insistence, however, is expected to be cautious and prudent, latent and implicit rather than direct or haughty. In fervent communities that basic truth needs seldom be mentioned and emphasized. It seems evident to everybody.

The last thing a saintly superior would consider is the subjects' favor and love, obtained by yielding to all their demands and wishes, whether justified and reasonable or not. Superiors so acting through human weakness had better be mindful of these words of the Apostle: "If I did yet please men, I should not be the servant of Christ." (*Gal.* 1:10). In fact, it is impossible for the superiors to meet all the wishes of their subjects. Fortunately enough, many superiors have learned from Our Lord, "The Delight of Mankind," how to refuse in so a charitable manner

as to prevent at least bitter feelings in the heart
of the disappointed petitioner. This practical wisdom, however, is brought about by an intensive
spiritual life and true union with God. The very
fact of the superior's sanctity—a fact which is
inevitably noticed by the subjects—makes submission easier and prevents excessive discontent
in the case of refusal. For, everybody is convinced that the saintly superior is activated by
objective, sublime motives.

Enlightened superiors are perfectly aware of
their special responsibility for the obedience of
the subjects, aware, likewise, of the difficulties
the subjects have in always subordinating their
will. Therefore, they anxiously avoid everything
that is liable to make obedience harder. Nay, they
take all possible measures to ease the yoke of
obedience for subjects. Unless special reasons forbid, they are wont to explain to the community
the motives or the reasons for certain burden-
some directions. And instead of giving harsh
orders, they will make their demands in the form
of requests or wishes. Of course, no prudent subject will be mistaken as to the binding character
of such cautious and prudent injunctions. These
charitable orders will be better obeyed than ruth-
less demands.

While the subjects are not obliged to inquire
whether each and every command of a superior
is objectively conformable with the Will of God,

but have, instead, to submit to all orders given them—superiors, on the contrary, are not free of this obligation. They must see to it that their decisions actually correspond to the wishes of the Divine Heart. Otherwise, they will be guilty of opposition to the Will of God. As subjects are to obey because the Will of God is revealed to them in the decisions of their superiors, so the latter are bound in conscience to adjust their demands, as best they can, to the objective good pleasure of God. They can ascertain the real Will of God by governing their community accurately according to the principles of holy prudence, according to the community's rule, and in strict compliance with all the directions of higher authorities. They may be mistaken in particular cases, but if they try to act in this manner, they are justified before God. It would be an unpardonable mistake on the part of a superior to fancy that he is free to present whatever he pleases as the real Will of God. He will render an account to God for every command issued at any time to his community.

Without question, subjects are bound to obedience without regard to the shortcomings in the methods applied by their superiors in governing the community. This, however, does not relieve the superiors of their heavy responsibility to use prudence, legality and general correctness in the orders issued and in their administration as a whole. No wonder, then, that many Saints have declined superiorship as long as they possibly could, using various and ingenious means to be spared that responsibility.

Between the religious superiors on the one hand, and their subjects on the other hand, a kind of holy emulation should take place in regard to the Holy Will of God and obedience. While subjects really abandoned to God will refrain from any form of criticism in matters of obedience, except when they certainly and evidently are entitled to make opposition, perfect and saintly superiors will scrupulously examine their particular directions and their general methods as well, to make sure that they are governing their flock in the spirit of Jesus, the Supreme and Divine Head of all communities. To secure their own conscience as to this point, such superiors avail themselves of the assistance of spiritual direction. If they constantly and seriously do this, regardless of all objections launched against them, they have nothing to fear on the day of their judgment, even after many years of superiorship.

A reliable sign of perfect superiorship consists in unrestricted and willing subordination of a superior both to Canon Law, to the Community's rule, and to all regulations of the higher authorities. Failing this, the unfaithful superior should not be surprised by the recalcitrant attitude of his or her subjects. Human weakness resorts only too easily and too often to the pretext in matters of obedience, that superiors should be the first to obey before they insist upon obedience on the part of their subjects. Though the excuse of subjects is unwarranted and vain in such circumstances, still the unfaithful superiors are partially responsible for the disorders creeping into their community.

To be fully entitled to refer to the Holy Will of God in his directions and precepts, a religious superior should be animated with a genuine, tender and practical devotion to this Adorable Will. He must wholeheartedly love the Divine Will. He should be enthusiastic about it. He should be the first to practice what he teaches.

22

ABOUT SOME UNFATHOMABLE
DESIGNS OF DIVINE PROVIDENCE

The history of mankind is filled with mysteries. Some details of our individual life bear characteristics of mystery, as well, and we wonder why Divine Providence has not preserved us from certain physical or moral evils. On the one hand, we face the indisputable truth that God is Love and infinite Goodness, and on the other hand, we know that suffering is the daily bread of man, of whole nations. And what is even more surprising, both the guilty and the innocent nations (or individuals) are subject to all kinds of affliction. There is not clear evidence of justice, according to human standards, in the history of mankind. Materialistic and godless people seem to have specious pretexts for their satanic theories.

The designs of Divine Providence seem even more impenetrable when the problem of human salvation is considered. True, the Son of God has come upon earth to redeem mankind by His teachings, His toils, His Passion and His death.

But before His Incarnation countless generations lived upon earth in spiritual darkness and in the shadow of death, and their knowledge of the Creator and of man's relationship to Him was very scant and vague. And in our day, almost two thousand years since the Redemption has been accomplished, there are more souls living outside the Church of God than within this Ark of Salvation. While Christian souls are flooded with the most precious supernatural favors and graces, millions of heathens are living in subnormal conditions, like disinherited children of the Heavenly Father. . .

In fine, appalling crimes and wrongs are committed almost daily against innocent people, and human justice is unable to prevent or adequately and promptly to punish these iniquities. Many victims of cruel persecution cry out for justice to God, but only in rare instances does God deign directly to intervene for the benefit of the innocent. It is understandable, then, that some people, fundamentally good and loving God, eventually become discouraged and disappointed in their confidence in Divine Providence. They are often exposed to the danger of moral shipwreck.

In the light of these and similar facts, man's nature is inclined to become melancholic and pessimistic.

Fortunately enough, a great many Christians,

who are most enlightened and competent, do not share this pessimistic viewpoint in regard to the fate of mankind, of nations, and of individuals. Their childlike, boundless confidence in God remains intact even in the face of the most tragic disasters permitted by God. How do they manage to preserve peace of heart? Are they able to explain, if only to themselves, the mysteries of Divine Providence? And, if so, what are the principles and the basic truths upon which they build their unshakable faith and confidence and love?

First of all, enlightened souls will never claim the right of grasping and fathoming all the designs of God, who is infinite Majesty and Wisdom, while man is but nothingness and corruption. To claim such a prerogative would amount to satanic pride, which might bring about the spirit of revolt against the Creator. A god whose nature, whose designs and authority over the world should present no mystery, would obviously not be the True and Living God. Since an infinite gulf separates God and man, since man is less than a speck of dust before his Creator, and since God is the absolute plenitude of Truth, of Good and of Beauty, how could this miserable creature comprehend God and His works? This humble estimation of one's nothingness before God must be the starting point of all inquiries into God's eternal designs and into the mysteries of Divine Providence.

Secondly, in keeping with sound reason, and with revealed religion, we must unhesitatingly and wholeheartedly adhere to the dogma that whatever God disposes is good and just and holy, and that even the permissive Will of God is to be accepted, adored and loved without reservation, regardless of all the doubts that assail our mind. Will anybody maintain that God is obliged to apologize to His creatures for the methods and manner of His rule? Any kind of criticism of God, of His designs or dispositions is obviously nonsense. Unless a soul, blinded by satanic pride, presumes to refer to God as equal to equal.

Thirdly, the whole history of mankind, its relationship to God, its destiny and obligations on earth—and likewise, the supreme end of every human soul and her condition in the present life—must be taken as presented by Divine revelation. That is to say, that our earthly life must be viewed as a preparatory stage of our existence for eternity. Then, and only then will our mind be able to seize the true sense of human life, and the purpose of all afflictions, sufferings and trials sent or permitted by God. Unbelievers who refuse to recognize even such evident truths as the existence of God, and take no account at all of the doctrine revealed by God, in reference to human sufferings, will inevitably find the history of mankind an embarrassing puzzle, a tragicomedy, if not a nonsense. . . But they are inexcusable, since the sun of Divine truth shines over them ever so brightly.

Souls who accept the three basic truths explained above may hope for abundant supernatural light to understand more and more the mysteries of Divine Providence. Provided they pray very often and with profound humility, they will see and feel God's fatherly hand and boundless love, even in the most excruciating trials visited upon individuals or nations. They will easily surmise what designs God may have in particular instances of suffering sent by His Providence. And since every sort of earthly affliction is a real boon in the supernatural sense, and since no one is denied the necessary grace of God to bear his cross, if only he prays for Divine assistance, the humble children of God will seldom be confused in the face of actual sufferings or disasters. They will sincerely and lovingly praise God for everything.

Not even the fate of the most abandoned people like savages living in African jungles, will disturb the inner peace and confidence of enlightened and humble souls. They are convinced that even these poor creatures are taken care of by Divine Providence. To avoid eternal damnation, they need only to follow their poorly instructed conscience, and serve God as best they can. For, no one can doubt that God's omnipotence and wisdom has more than sufficient means and ways to save all souls on earth. How and when God's mercy will complete that work, no one is entitled to question and to know. One thing, however, is absolutely sure: No soul on earth will ever be rejected and damned by God without its own fault. If certain innocent creatures, like unbaptized children, cannot attain supernatural bliss and union with God in Heaven, they will certainly enjoy natural happiness, by praising and loving God on a natural level. And even this kind of happiness is an immense and undeserved gift of Divine Goodness.

The more a soul advances upon the way of sanctity, the deeper her understanding of the mysteries of Divine Providence. Facts and problems which in times past may have utterly disturbed the soul's peace and confidence in God will constitute new incentive for more ardent love toward God, after the soul has drawn closer to God and is now able to see things, so to say, in God, and from the standpoint of God.

In fine, once the veil of faith is definitely lifted, and a soul joins the Elect in Heaven to contemplate the Blessed Trinity face to face, all the mysteries of Divine Providence will be revealed to her. And then every detail contained in them will produce in her heart new transports of love.

23

ADHERENCE TO THE WILL OF GOD MAKES CHARACTER INVINCIBLE

A firm, unwavering character is commonly regarded as a gift of inestimable worth in man. A reliable character is essential to become a useful member of human society. A very firm character is necessary to advance in Christian and religious virtue and perfection. And in fine, to become a saint takes a character of superhuman fortitude.

A religious who wishes to achieve great things for God's glory and love, by sanctifying himself and assisting other people on the road to Heaven, must rid himself of ordinary human weakness and softness. He must use supernatural means to make his character firm and solid. A soft life can never be a virtuous, and much less, a saintly one. It amounts to plain egotism when a soul is unable to spend itself for unselfish motives and for the benefit of others. Christian perfection, which means steady progress in the love of God and of our neighbor, demands many acts of self-denial and countless sacrifices. But no soft and weak character is able to walk this heroic road.

An impetuous, impulsive temper should not be mistaken for a firm character, since temper is a quality of the sensual part of human nature, whereas character is inherent in the human will. It is a spiritual reality. Its firmness is by no means dependent upon a man's impetuosity. Experience rather proves the contrary, namely, that a temperament balanced by self-control is more indicative of moral energy and determination, or real character, than a violent nature. Character can be defined shortly as a habit of living up to the principles one has recognized as true and binding, while disregarding the difficulties and reasons to the contrary.

A religious soul shows real and firm character by carrying out in practice all the rules of perfection she has learned from the Saints and from Jesus Christ Himself. The more consistent and persevering she is in her supernatural way of life, the stronger her character. Frequent and regrettable as her daily failures may be, she must be credited with a firm character, nevertheless, if only she shows herself determined not to give up the spiritual combat. On the contrary, acts of virtue that are performed only sporadically, very irregularly, constitute no sufficient evidence for a firm and perfect character.

Instances of character which can be called

unshakable and unconquerable are found in people who rely, in theory and in practice, upon God Omnipotent. The remarkable consistency of some godless individuals in pursuing their wretched goals deserves rather the name of demoniac doggedness than that of character. For they are not motivated by sublime principles, but rather by an unreasonable, stubborn self-will. Perfect character must participate in God's infinite sanctity, as it shares in an infinitesimal degree in Divine Omnipotence.

To rely upon God in the religious life and to strive for religious sanctity amounts to union with the Will of God, with His good pleasure, with His adorable, eternal designs. Consequently, the more sincere and profound a soul's devotion to the Will of God, the firmer her character will prove in daily life. Experience supplies ample evidence of the truth of this statement. Are not saintly souls blamed at times for being self-willed and obstinate? Actually, they are but consistent and adamant in their fidelity to God and to their obligations. The Will of God constitutes the only rule of life for them. And come what may, they are determined not to deviate from that rule whenever God's good pleasure is unquestionable. Yes, their character is unconquerable.

Whoever is aware of the fact that his aims and strivings originate in personal likes and whims rather than in God's objective Will, cannot but feel hesitant in his undertakings. He cannot hope for the Divine blessing. His conscience being uneasy, he must be exposed again and again to attacks of despondency and disgust. Since he sees no objective sublime motives for his exertions, he has to rely upon himself, his human weakness and misery, his unreasonable self-will—a rather discouraging situation. No wonder, then, that souls too little interested in the Will of God resemble in their lives—"reeds shaken with the wind." (*Matt.* 11:7).

When during the Middle Ages Christian armies were organized to free the Holy Land from the yoke of the infidel, the slogan most effective for the purpose was: "God wills it!" Evidently, Christian masses were particularly receptive to this motive. It proved to be a source of supernatural power that enabled the Crusaders to perform the most heroic exploits for God's glory and for the welfare of Christianity. How much more should religious souls, called to perfection and striving for it, feel enthusiastic about God's Will. Tender devotion to the Will of God should permeate them with the spirit of indomitable fortitude in combatting Satan, the wicked world, and their own inordinate passions. Indeed, those fostering that devotion greatly resemble valiant knights of God.

The virtue of supernatural fortitude being dependent upon our growing adherence to the

Will of God, an important practical question arises in this connection. How can a religious ascertain whether her devotion to the Divine Will is developing, not only theoretically and in the sphere of sentiments, but actually in daily life? According to the explanations given in the preceding chapters, a concise answer should read as follows:

Once a soul striving for religious sanctity has managed to establish perfect order in her external life, that is to say, having accustomed herself to faithful observance of her vows and of her religious rule, let her sincerely, assiduously, unhesitatingly strive to attain such a degree of virtue and sanctity as she is able to understand and feels able to pursue with the grace of God, instead of restricting herself to obligatory perfection. Then, and only then, will her compliance with the Holy Will of God prove unquestionable and perfect in every regard. And only under this condition her character, her determination in the service of God will grow firmer and firmer, until she is—as far as possible on earth—confirmed in her fidelity and her abandonment to God.

Let us add here that there is no other way of advancing in Christian fortitude and sanctity than that of cheerful adherence to the Will of God. It is a hard, toilsome, often heroic way . . . But why delude oneself that it is possible to reach the same goal of union with God and perfect happiness in God by wandering along comfortable byways? Our disappointment on the threshold of Eternity would in such a case be complete and bitter.

Wise strategy makes it imperative to attack the foe at the point which seems to be more dangerous. Now, our self-will undoubtedly is the arch-enemy of our sanctification and our future glory. Let us valiantly attack the very center of his frontline, despite all obstacles and difficulties, by wholehearted and childlike adherence to God's good pleasure and Will. Delaying the decisive combat on the way to Heaven and sanctity serves no useful purpose. It only makes the striving for perfection the harder, and the final result more doubtful. At any cost, therefore, let us embrace the Will of God with ever increasing love, and carry it out despite all the efforts of Hell to block our way.

A soul unreservedly and lovingly devoted to the Will of God accomplishes more for God's glory and for the welfare of souls than whole armies of social or religious workers who rely chiefly upon human means and human ability.

24

LOVE OF THE DIVINE WILL, THE SWEETEST CONSOLATION IN PAINFUL TRIALS

Imagine, Dear Soul, an innocent sufferer who has been accused of crimes he never committed. Because of false testimony and circumstantial evidence all against him, he is sentenced to life-imprisonment. A young man of thirty years, just about to start a profitable business and a happy career. With heart-rending sobs and all in tears, he says goodbye to wife and children before he is taken to the rigid seclusion of his prison cell.

For hours he is not able to control his feelings. Streams of tears are running down his emaciated countenance. His heart is completely broken. In the name of justice, a terrible wrong has been inflicted upon this innocent man... Then, maybe as a result of diabolical temptation, despair and inner revolt set in. The poor victim of injustice is about to curse his fate, to curse human justice, to murmur against Divine Providence. Fortunately, however, he is a good Christian. He has learned to turn to God in critical moments of life. So he feels himself urged to pray, and in fact starts praying wholeheartedly. "Our Father Who art in Heaven...Thy Will be done"...his lips whisper again and again, as if under an irresistible insistence of Divine grace...And suddenly he seems to awaken from a deep slumber. "Why this despondence and revolt of mine?"—he asks of himself. "Am I not in the hands of God? Is not everything that comes upon me the Will of God? Is it not permitted by Him for my greater merit and glory in eternity? Yes, yes...Thy Will be done, O Lord, on earth as it is in Heaven."

Thus the afflicted man prays. As a result, heavenly peace descends upon him and fills his heart. He feels resigned to comply with the Will of God, even if it means unmerited imprisonment for life. After long hours of humble and childlike prayer, after repeatedly consulting spiritual books, as he was wont to do for years, the poor sufferer begins supernaturally to love his fate. He realizes the similarity of his sentence to the unjust condemnation of Jesus, Innocence personified. He reads and studies the Holy Gospel, especially the chapters on the Lord's Passion and death. In fine, he cannot resist the Divine inspiration to pray as Jesus did: "Father, forgive them, for they know not what they do." (*Luke* 23:34)...But his prayer of preference is the short aspiration: "O Lord, Thy Will be done!". . . He is peaceful and happy now, despite occasional assaults of sadness and desolation.

Instances of this kind are not uncommon in Christian society wherever religion is not only a theory or venerable tradition, but where it is practiced and lived.

According to the consensus of ascetical and mystical writers, those privileged souls called by God to high degrees of prayer, to real contemplation and to close union with Him, must during this mortal life, pass through a furnace of appalling inner trials, through periods of complete spiritual darkness, aridity, and apparent abandonment by God. Their moral sufferings are comparable to those of the Poor Souls in Purgatory; in a certain restricted sense, they resemble the inner torments of the damned in Hell. This is true at least of those who feel themselves forsaken by God. And yet, none of these chosen friends of God are, indeed, unhappy. Not even those who cannot help praying with Jesus: "My God, my God, why hast Thou forsaken me?" They find real peace, supernatural, Divine peace, in their union with the Will of God. And where there is peace, there is happiness.

Jesus hanging upon the Cross, immersed in an ocean of humiliation and suffering, both physical and moral, was not unhappy even for a moment. For, God can never feel unhappy. Unhappiness starts where revolt against some inevitable necessity sets in. Now, the human Will of Jesus was always and everywhere united with the Will of His Heavenly Father, and that in the highest possible degree. Not only was actual revolt absolutely impossible with Jesus, but even the least shade of opposition to the good pleasure of the Father at any moment of His earthly life. Hence, it is true without any restriction whatsoever that our suffering Lord enjoyed real and full inner happiness during His whole Passion and at the moment of His death. For, happiness means peace in God.

This "peace in God" is the unquestionable share of the chosen but suffering souls mentioned above, as experienced directors of conscience admit. The lower faculties of their nature, the senses and the body itself, may sustain untold torments. However, the heart, the will, the very center of the soul, rest in God who is Peace, Joy and Happiness. Those saintly sufferers, by the grace of God, comply more perfectly with the Divine Will than human words can tell. They are immersed in the Will of God. No wonder, then, that they suffer, so to say, in an atmosphere of heavenly bliss. A mysterious, Divine paradox...

To increase your devotion and love for the Will of God, stop for awhile at the gates of Purgatory. No man on earth can form an adequate conception of the punishment which the inmates of Purgatory endure, particularly as the term to serve in that penitentiary of Divine Justice may extend beyond hundreds and thousands of years for certain souls. The punishment inflicted upon sinners who have been saved from Hell only by a miracle of Divine mercy, at the last moment of their life, and consequently had no chance to atone for their immense and innumerable faults on earth, probably will differ from the torments of Hell only in duration. They will not last forever...Despite this appalling fate, there is no despair in Purgatory. This place of untold suffering is filled with an atmosphere of peace. The Poor Souls there enjoy a certain kind of happiness. It is not happiness in the full sense of the term, but it is a condition approaching actual happiness, much more than the moral dispositions and sentiments of some people on earth who consciously revolt against their Maker.

Yes, the Poor Souls in Purgatory, in a certain sense, feel happy. They cannot but feel happy, on account of the fact that they love the Will of God without reservation.

Imagine the gates of Purgatory wide open, with no guards to prevent possible escape from that terrible prison. But you would never see any of the Poor Souls even try to escape. For all of them embrace the Will of God with such an immense love, bitter and excruciating as that Will is, that they prefer to have their punishment increased a thousandfold than to make the slightest opposition against God and His infinite Justice. Therefore, there is not even the shadow of despair to be found in Purgatory.

And finally, Hell is Hell chiefly because of the revolt against God of all the wicked creatures confined there. Never imagine the damned in Hell deploring their past life and the sins committed against God. No, there is not a trace of contrition in any damned creature. Revolt against God and boundless hatred of His eternal Justice is the preoccupation and the actual life of all wicked in Hell. Thus, they must be unhappy beyond human expression and conception. And since these wretched creatures stubbornly adhere to that hatred and revolt, they do not deserve the least sympathy.

You are, Dear Soul, in need of consolation in your present life. You could hardly bear an existence void of every consolation. According to the designs of Divine Providence, life on earth, though a period of trial and struggle, is a time to gather merits for eternity. However, our struggles may be occasionally relieved and sweetened by natural and supernatural consolations. So you are right when seeking consolation. But never forget the truth voiced by all the Saints of God and confirmed by experience, that there is no consolation on earth or in Heaven comparable to that resulting from wholehearted, loving union with the Holy Will of God.

– 25 –

IN THE FACE OF DEATH
LET US LOVINGLY UNITE
WITH THE WILL OF GOD

Our whole life on earth ought to be a preparation for the moment of death, since then our fate for all eternity will be decided. "What shall it profit a man, if he gain the whole world, and suffer the loss of his soul?" (*Mark* 8:36). This maxim is so simple, clear and convincing, as to make any explanation or demonstration superfluous. It takes only a moment of thinking to realize its grave, inevitable meaning.

For a religious soul, faithful to all obligations and entirely abandoned to God, preparation for death does not mean repeated and too anxious examination of conscience, since it has been regulated and set at rest. It rather means drawing nearer and nearer to God, through the loving union with the Will of God. If this union has with time reached a high degree of perfection, then death itself holds no excessive fear. It means rather a transition from earthly misery to heavenly bliss.

Genuine and profound devotion to the Will of God is not only a condition of a saintly and very meritorious death, but besides, it rids the most timid and pusillanimous soul of her excessive apprehensions and scruples. Hence she can hope to die in a childlike transport of Divine love, and in such a heavenly atmosphere there is no room for excessive worry or cowardly fear.

So, then, beginning today, let us view our death, whether near or far off, as the Holy Will of God, who has determined the moment of our death and all its circumstances from all eternity. No other pious exercise can be more profitable to our spiritual welfare than this form of meditation and abandonment to God. It may radically transform and advance our whole spiritual life.

First of all, let us leave the moment of our death entirely to the good pleasure of our Heavenly Father. It is not our business. After all, the actual value and usefulness of our earthly existence is not dependent so much upon the length of our life as upon our more or less perfect compliance with God's good pleasure in our thoughts, feelings, strivings, words, deeds and our sufferings. The Little Flower of Lisieux has given more glory and love to God, and has helped to save or sanctify more souls during her twenty-four years of life, than many apostolic laborers in the course of fifty or sixty years.

Do not presume to think that God is in need of your work for the spreading of His kingdom on earth. No, He does not need anybody's help in realizing His eternal designs. And if He deigns to use human work for that purpose, He certainly can raise up hosts of willing apostles and social workers, at the proper time. He knows what is most conducive to His glory, to the salvation and sanctification of souls. Is He not able "to raise up children to Abraham"—of stones, as Our Lord put it? (*Matt.* 3:9). Your work in the vineyard of the Lord, undoubtedly, is of immense importance, and it constitutes one of the essential conditions of your sanctification, but only as far as God clearly manifests His Will either by obedience or some other unquestionable sign. After all, God can have His full glory apart from your endeavors. So your premature death—if this term should be used at all—will not necessarily prove detrimental to the glory of God.

Willing acceptance of a premature death is essential to genuine sanctity; on the contrary, every form of opposition to the Divine Will demeans that sanctity. But great sanctity characterized by supernatural heroism implies, besides, a sincere longing for an early death. High sanctity and perfect union with God can be achieved only through an immense love toward God. This love will not fail to engender in the soul a growing desire for Heaven, a secret longing for the

Beatific Vision and final union with God. Complete absence of such a mystical yearning after God makes high sanctification rather doubtful.

The assumption, however, that the mentioned longing for an early entrance to Heaven should grow stronger and stronger, so as to resemble eventually a feverish, uneasy desire for an early death, is a mistake. Absolute compliance with the Will of God must always be and forever remain the supreme law of sanctity. In other words, a saintly soul may and should sincerely long for Heaven, but her desire to unite her will with God's good pleasure must be a thousand-fold stronger. In fact, this desire must unquestionably and entirely dominate her whole existence. The desire of Heaven may never oppose a soul's devotion to the Will of God. It must rather be a fruit and a supplement of that absolutely essential devotion.

Never give in, Dear Soul, to pusillanimous apprehensions, which may assail you whenever the thought of your death occurs to your mind. You may fear all the doubts, temptations and sufferings that as a rule accompany the final moments of human life. Beware, we insist, of this pusillanimity! If God is with you, what kind of harm can you suffer? "Though I should walk in the midst of the shadow of death, I will fear no evils, for thou art with me" (*Ps.* 22:4)—this should be your incessant prayer. Now, if you are unconditionally abandoned to the Will of God, whatever the circumstances of your life, if you love this Adorable Will with your whole heart, if you sincerely and assiduously try day by day to be interested in nothing but the Holy Will of God and His good pleasure, then your passage into eternity will undoubtedly be marked by sweet confidence in God and by heavenly peace. You have nothing to fear. This statement is not an arbitrary assumption. It is based upon countless instances of the very happy, peaceful death of saintly souls. They were animated by seraphic love of the Divine Will, and were wont daily to abandon themselves to God without regarding the sufferings and afflictions which would presumably accompany their last moments of life.

No, no! You cannot be deceived in your confidence in God! Shake off, therefore, all pusillanimous feelings and thoughts! Immerse yourself deeper and deeper into Divine love, into the Adorable Will of God, into humble, childlike prayer, and death will appear to you rather as a supernatural boon than as a dreadful catastrophe.

No one can promise you that you will joyfully pass through the gate of death, in the human sense of the word. It is rather to be assumed that your deathbed will be your cross and your Calvary. Nay, if you are called to high sanctity and very close union with God, your last moments may resemble those of Our Crucified Lord. Your physical and spiritual sufferings may be very great. What does it matter, though, to be submerged in an ocean of suffering, if Jesus and Mary are with you? Their presence will guarantee your soul's safety and perseverance. And the very remembrance that you are suffering as they themselves did suffer on Calvary, cannot but fill your heart with heavenly consolation. And this excruciating trial will last only for a short time. Then Heaven will open and you will enter the final union with God, with His Holy Will, in everlasting peace and bliss.

Adopt, Dear Soul, the heroic practice of the Saints, daily to submit in advance, seriously, unreservedly and lovingly to all the afflictions which are to accompany your death. Do it by kissing your crucifix or pressing it to your heart, and by imploring Jesus to bestow upon you all necessary graces. If you have spent your life in union with the Will of God, and in humble prayer, then you too will die as the Saints died, in sweet confidence, in peace, in a childlike transport of love.

26

THE ELECT IN HEAVEN LOVINGLY AND BLISSFULLY IMMERSED IN THE HOLY WILL OF GOD

To unite with the Will of God means, for the average Christian, submission to the Divine decrees in adversities, afflictions and sufferings. Few people realize that our union with the Divine Will is not a temporary obligation, restricted to the period of earthly pilgrimage, spiritual combat and gathering merits for eternity, but is to last forever. In fact, this union cannot be complete and perfect before we are admitted to the Beatific Vision in Heaven. Then we shall be immersed—more and more, so to say, in the Adorable Will of God, as we shall be able increasingly to fathom the mysteries of Divinity.

Our union with God's Will and good pleasure in Heaven will constitute the main source of our happiness throughout eternity, as submission to His Divine decrees on earth is the surest guarantee of inner peace. Is this assertion arbitrary or too far-fetched? Are we in Heaven to continue a life of self-immolation for the glory of God, instead of enjoying the fruits of our sacrifices offered to God on earth? No, no! Our treatise does not imply any form of painful sacrifice in Heaven. But it does imply perfect abandonment to God and a kind of blissful self-forgetfulness of all the Elect in Heaven.

Self-forgetfulness in Heaven?—you may ask. Heaven is the place of boundless happiness. How, then, can a soul be expected to forget her personal interests there and still enjoy unlimited bliss? And yet, in a certain form, self-forgetfulness takes place in Heaven—as a result of love toward God. Is it not essential to any kind of genuine love to forget one's self in order to live for the person beloved? Love of God, the most perfect and most powerful affection imaginable, is no exception in this regard. On the contrary, supreme, seraphic love toward God implies self-forgetfulness in the highest degree. Though, it may not be understood as a loss or a sacrifice on the part of the loving soul. It constitutes rather the perfecting element in the soul's heavenly bliss.

To a certain extent, our experience during the present life confirms the assertion that self-forgetfulness is bound to enhance rather than to restrict our happiness. Is not every generous sacrifice in favor of our neighbor connected with a special moral delight? And is it not a fact commonly known to souls abandoned to God, that self-forgetfulness, resulting in many spontaneous sacrifices for love of God gives a foretaste of Heaven on earth? No wonder, then, that a certain kind of self-forgetfulness is to continue in Heaven.

The principle of all principles concerning our relationship to God is this external, immutable truth: Man exists for God, not God for man. That is to say: God is and must remain forever the supreme End of man, of all his thoughts, desires, strivings, and deeds, indeed, of his whole existence in time and in eternity. And man is perfect only insofar as he lives up to this eternal rule. By the same token, the happiness of a human soul increases or diminishes, as she adheres, in theory and in practice, more or less consistently to God's absolute supremacy in the universe, and particularly in her individual existence. Hence, the state of the Elect in Heaven is one of definite perfection and of unlimited, complete happiness, because they are living in God, and for God. Their individual existence is by no means extinguished, nor in the least impaired by this fact. On the contrary, it is as highly intensified and perfected as is possible for created beings.

How is this life of the Elect, in God and for God, to be understood and imagined?

The answer of Catholic theology to this mystical question reads as follows: The Blessed Souls in Heaven see God face to face, in virtue of a transcendent grace of God called "the light of glory." Without being able fully to comprehend God, on account of His infinite perfections, they gradually acquire a better knowledge of the mysteries of Divine Existence. They understand in part the supreme mystery of One God in Three Persons, and the mutual relationship of the Divine Persons, as well. What fills the hearts of all the Elect with inconceivable joy and bliss is, above all, God's eternal and infinite Beatitude; a happiness infinitely beyond all possible forms of created happiness. This Beatitude is not something added to God's Existence, but it is God Himself. It consists in the absolute Fullness of Good, Truth and Beauty—in possessing in Himself all conceivable objects of complacency. Being omniscient and infinitely wise, God is infinite Intelligence. He is not, however, abstract, cold intelligence, He is a living and loving Intelligence. He is Love infinite, as He is Intelligence infinite. And both His Love and Intelligence are identical with His Essence and Existence. God's beatitude, to use our inadequate, poor language, is realized by Love, by that incomprehensible, infinite Love which unites the Father, the Son and the Holy Ghost in one indivisible Divinity. God's Beatitude is infinite, because the mutual Love of the Father, of the Son and of the Holy Ghost is infinite. Thus the Divine Will, the eternal, immanent or intrinsic Will of the Blessed Trinity is realized with absolute, infinite perfection.

All these mysteries of Divine Existence and Divine Beatitude, of the eternal, immanent Will of God, of God's complacency in Himself and His glory, and in fine of God's good pleasure in His external works—constitute the main object of contemplation for the Elect in Heaven. They are incomparably more interested in God's glory, complacency and Beatitude, than with anything related to their own happiness. They enjoy their full personal happiness, but chiefly because it results in God's glory and contributes, as it were, to God's own Beatitude. Thus it is true that the Blessed Souls in Heaven live much more in God, through God and for God, than for themselves. God's Will, good pleasure, and complacency is what substantially constitutes their eternal bliss.

The joys of Paradise, doubtless, correspond to all the noble aspirations and yearnings of human nature. Consequently, many additional joys and consolations are allotted to the Elect in Heaven. All the desires of their hearts will be met. However, Heaven is Heaven, first of all, on account of the Divine Beatitude, or boundless and bottomless ocean of bliss, which the Elect contemplate with increasing delight. They can no longer doubt that God's Will and good pleasure is realized in full measure and to the highest degree. So, instead of longingly praying as they did on earth: Thy Will be done, O Lord...they rather triumphantly repeat the doxology: Glory be to

the Father and to the Son and to the Holy
Ghost. . .They feel happy beyond expression and
conception, as the Will of God, their only Love,
is done now in Heaven, in the most perfect
manner.

Do you surmise now, Dear Soul, why the Saints
were so enthusiastic about the Will of God during their earthly life? Enlightened by grace, they
were partially able to imagine that blissful existence which awaited them in Heaven. And
prompted by Divine inspirations, they resolved
to begin this life of union with the Will of God,
here on earth. For, they knew only too well that
the degree of union with God in eternity, and
consequently, the degree of glory and happiness,
would depend upon the soul's fidelity to the grace
of God during this life.

In fact, every soul faithful to God and docile
to all inspirations of the Holy Ghost is anxiously
intent upon complying with God's good pleasure even in minute things. She feels very uneasy
in conscience whenever she must fear that she
has even slightly opposed the Divine Will. Thus
cooperating with the grace of God, she sooner
or later reaches a high degree of union with the
Will of Divine Trinity. She feels inflamed with
love toward that Adorable Will. In fine, she gives
up all other desires and strivings, to unite herself
as perfectly as possible in the Holy Will of God.

27

LET OUR INCESSANT AND
BELOVED PRAYER BE:
THY WILL BE DONE, O LORD!

Our Most Holy Redeemer Himself has made it clear that to enter Heaven, formal prayer is not sufficient, but that we must also do the Will of God. "Not every one that saith to me, Lord, Lord, shall enter into the kingdom of heaven: but he that doth the will of my Father who is in heaven, he shall enter into the kingdom of heaven." (*Matt.* 7:21).

This Holy Will is manifest to everybody who sincerely wishes to know and see it. The Divine Commandments, the precepts and regulations of Holy Church, the civil law, the special duties of our state or profession, Divine trials coming upon us in the form of physical or moral sufferings, and especially the demands of holy obedience, and in fine, the secret inspirations and promptings of the Holy Ghost, reveal in detail God's Holy Will for us. There is no moment in our life when we could say that we do not know what God wants us to do. Even if the real or objective Will of God would seem doubtful, we are aware of the fact that God wants us to do what we sincerely believe to be in accord with His good pleasure.

In favorable circumstances it may prove easy to comply with God's good pleasure, so as to make us cheerfully meet our obligations. At other times, however, and in fact, in most instances, complying with the Divine Will implies serious exertion, self-denial, sacrifice—in certain cases even heroic self-forgetfulness. Our thoughts turn as if spontaneously to God's Holy Will at the more difficult moments of our life. We instinctively feel that recalling God's Will cannot but encourage and strengthen our soul. Blessed are they, indeed, who have made it a habit, a second nature, always to repeat that simple and childlike aspiration: "Thy Will be done, O Lord". . .They have found the mystic key to profound happiness on earth, to higher and greater sanctity, to inconceivable bliss in eternity.

"Thy Will be done". . .such should be your morning prayer. It should be on your lips when your work is hard and wearisome. The remembrance of the Will of God certainly is able to make your task lighter and sweeter. When hardships, adversities, failures, humiliations, overwhelm you, remember you can transform them into precious boons, real graces of God, provided you view them as God's good pleasure. Even painful sufferings will lose their most excruciating sting as a result of that little prayer.

"Thy Will be done". . .with these words you should begin your daily work. Say it with childlike love toward God present at your side, nay, dwelling within your heart. For, according to the degree of your love, your merits will increase or diminish.

"Thy Will be done". . .should be said as often as possible in the course of your work. Should you forget about this little aspiration for long stretches of time, then boredom, weariness or despondency cannot but assail you again and again. Your recollection in God will then fade rapidly.

"Thy Will be done". . .this prayer should be in your heart during your short "spiritual rests" when at a free moment you either call on Jesus in the Tabernacle, or inwardly converse with the Blessed Trinity at the place of your work. No other prayer can so gladden the Divine Heart as that prayer which was so characteristic of the inner life of Our Lord.

"Thy Will be done". . .will prove all the more important to your peace and sanctification as often as you face humiliation in whatever form. This may happen when your personality or your achievements are slighted. It may result from misunderstanding your good intentions. Perhaps faults will be charged against you on groundless assumptions. Whatever it is, the suggested aspiration will enable you to keep humbly silent, as Jesus before Pilate's tribunal. You will even feel happy to share, if only in the lowest degree, the humiliations of the Son of God.

"Thy Will be done". . . is essential to your spiritual balance and to the peace of your heart at the hour of keen sufferings. Whether you are subject to a serious and dangerous disease or to embarrassing chronic ailments, make sure that you are complying with God's good pleasure by frequently repeating the above suggested prayer, at least in the depths of your heart.

"Thy Will be done" proves the only effective consolation in the hour of serious spiritual afflictions, doubts, aridity of heart, spiritual darkness, lack of pious sentiments, scrupulosity and the like. The more your spiritual agony resembles that of Jesus in Gethsemane, the oftener repeat with Him: "Thy Will be done, Father, not mine". . .

"Thy Will be done". . . in the face of approaching death—that is your best preparation not only for a happy but for a holy death. By an unrestricted and love-inspired abandonment to the Divine Will as to the moment of your death and all its circumstances, you are able to supplement all shortcomings of your religious sanctity. By a miracle of grace, this can be achieved even in few hours or moments.

Let it be the perpetual song of our soul: "Thy Will be done, O Lord—on earth as it is in Heaven." No life can be more sublime and more blissful than one of wholehearted union with the Holy Will of God.

Whoever has adequately grasped this truth, has penetrated the deepest mystery of the spiritual life and of sanctity.

Let, then, this aspiration: "Thy Will be done"—be the breath of your soul!...You need nothing else, besides that, for your complete sanctification.

Whether you say it orally or mentally, in the depths of your heart, is of secondary importance, provided your will is unconditionally abandoned to God. Once you have acquired the habit of adoring God's Will with childlike love in all details of your life, of embracing it the more affectionately the more it hurts your nature, the less you need to worry about the scarcity of time allotted to formal prayer, under religious obedience, and in the midst of your intense professional activity. You are praying all day. Acts of love toward God spring from your heart almost uninterruptedly. This is, undoubtedly, a very sublime form of prayer. It resembles deep contemplation, whose most essential element is seraphic love of God.

Take this royal way of sanctity, Dear Soul. Start today. At this very moment. God wills it. You will give to God the greatest possible glory. And you will become the happiest creature on earth.

We hope your cherished dream is to die as the Saints died—in a childlike transport of love toward God. If this is your supreme desire, exert yourself incessantly to unite your own will with the Will of God in everything. To satisfy God's good pleasure should be your only ideal and aspiration in life. This amounts to a genuine and very ardent love of God. Day by day you will draw nearer and nearer to the ideal of seraphic love toward God.

And as a result, your last thought, your last desire on earth, your last sentiment and your last spiritual exertion, perhaps, your last words, too, will be: "Thy Will be done, O my Jesus. . .Thy Will be done, now and forever. . .I love Thee, my God, I love Thee, I love Thee". . .This transport of love will constitute a real foretaste of eternal bliss.

If you have enjoyed this book, consider making your next selection from among the following . . .

Prices guaranteed through December 31, 1992.

Prices guaranteed through December 31, 1992.